The
CLASSIC
HERB GARDEN

Further Reading

Other books by *Remember When* include:

The Classic Allotment by Gordon Thorburn

Food Through the Ages by Anna Selby

Old-Fashioned Remedies from Arsenic to Gin by Dr Rob Hicks

Victorian Health Remedies by Dr Thomas Allinson, edited by Anna Selby

Coming soon:

Pubs and Their History by Gordon Thorburn

Foraging by Paul Chambers

Heal Your Dog the Natural Way by Richard Allport

The CLASSIC HERB GARDEN

GORDON THORBURN

First published in Great Britain in 2010 by
REMEMBER WHEN
an imprint of
Pen & Sword Books Ltd
47 Church Street
Barnsley
South Yorkshire
S70 2AS

Copyright © Gordon Thorburn, 2010

ISBN 978 1 84468 074 0

A CIP catalogue record for this book is
available from the British Library.

Printed and bound in Thailand by
Kyodo Nation Printing Services

Pen & Sword Books Ltd incorporates the imprints of
Pen & Sword Aviation, Pen & Sword Maritime, Pen & Sword Military,
Wharncliffe Local History, Pen & Sword Select, Pen & Sword Military Classics,
Leo Cooper, Remember When, Seaforth Publishing and Frontline Publishing

For a complete list of Pen & Sword titles please contact
PEN & SWORD BOOKS LIMITED
S70 2AS, England
l.co.uk
:o.uk

Contents

Acknowledgements

Many thanks to Sue Thorburn for her illustrations and to Sarah Cuttle for her help with plant identification. And thanks for the garlic, Fiona Cutting.

Photography by the author.
Special photography by Sarah Cuttle.

Author's note: this book is aimed at those who would grow herbs and who are interested in herbs in a general way. It is not a medicinal herbal. Any medicinal uses of herbs should be under supervision or with expert advice and proper research.

Some weomen we find, sprinkle the floures of cowslip with whyte wine and after still it and wash their faces with that water to drive wrinkles away and to make them fayre in the eyes of the worlde.

A New Herball, William Turner, 1508–1568.

Credited with magical powers as a restorative cosmetic, widely used as a basis for wine and featuring in all sorts of recipes from headache cures to minnow omelette, it is very sad that over-picking, along with changes in farming methods over the last fifty years, have made a once-plentiful plant into a near rarity.

And I serve the fairy queen,
To dew her orbs upon the green:
The cowslips tall her pensioners be;
In their gold coats spots you see;
Those be rubies, fairy favours,
In those freckles live their savours:
I must go seek some dew-drops here,
And hang a pearl in every cowslip's ear.

A Midsummer Night's Dream, William Shakespeare, 1564–1616.

Our city dames know well enough the ointment or distilled water [of cowslip flowers] adds to beauty or at least restores it when it is lost. An ointment being made with them taketh away spots and wrinkles of the skin, sunburnings and freckles.

The English Physician Enlarged, or the Herbal, Nicholas Culpeper, 1616–1654.

According to an old manuscript about magic, 'The Herb Pimpernel is good to prevent witchcraft, as Mother Bumby doth affirm.' This may be a disappointing view to those French dames who were rather hoping their pimpernel would work some witchcraft on their behalf. Mother Bumby, by the way, was the generalised, collective medieval name for those witches and wise-women who dispensed cures, spells, herbal lore and other forms of doctoring where there were no doctors, in return for a small fee.

As they used to say in the sixteenth and seventeenth centuries, because you're worth it.

'The distilled water or juice [of the scarlet pimpernel] is much celebrated by French dames to cleanse the skin from any roughness, deformity or discolourings thereof.' Nicholas Culpeper.

Chapter One

In the Beginning

We know what the ancient, literate civilisations did with herbs. They very kindly wrote it all down for us. But people had been aware of the properties of certain plants long, long before writing was invented. We can only speculate about the first, specific uses of herbs by the earliest humans, but we can say that herbs, as food, medicine and special helpmeet, were so closely intertwined with human evolution and development that we could never have got where we are without them.

Even the word has progressed in a fairly straight line through all that time, always with a 'b'. The earliest written evidence is from around 1500 BC. In Sanskrit, the parent language of Greek and Latin (and many, many others), the root of our word 'herb' is *bhar-*, to nourish, which morphed into the Greek *phorbê* and the old Latin *forbear*, meaning grass. By the time of classical Latin, the word had become *herba*, with a broader meaning including green vegetation, springing growth of leaf, green crop, and herb as we think of it now.

After the Latin word came the old French *erbe* and so into English, still with a more embracing meaning than now. In medieval times, an ordinary garden might have fifty different plants cultivated in it called herbs, pronounced 'erbs' until the nineteenth century, which explains why the Americans say it that way. All of the fifty, or more, were considered either essential or very important to nourishment and wellbeing, rather than merely decorative or flavoursome.

Today we tend to define 'herb' more narrowly, as a plant that has a use but is not one of our main food plants. We would say marjoram and St John's wort were herbs, but not cabbage. Would we call ground elder, nettle and chickweed herbs? We should, and later in the book we shall, but in our modern era we don't actually need to grow, for ourselves, any of these useful-but-not-mainstream plants. Why is that? What has happened to our relationship with something so intertwined with our own process of civilisation and so vital to it?

Now we are used to doctors who have medicines that work. If we feel unwell, we go to our general practitioner in expectation of the correct, functional, safe and preferably instant remedy. If we cut a finger we go to the cupboard for the Dettol and the Elastoplast. If we have backache from hard work, we get our beloved to rub on some Ibuleve. If we have toothache we call the dentist, make an appointment and meanwhile take a painkiller, such as paracetamol or Teacher's Highland Cream. If we pick up athlete's foot from the squash club showers, we go to the chemist's and buy the latest super-powerful fungicidal powder.

Assuming we are in reasonably good shape, we might decide to cook something for supper. In the kitchen, if we then find something smells a bit off, we'll throw it away. Some of us throw perfectly good food away on the day it passes its best before date. We might even throw away a little jar of dried marjoram, and go and buy another. If there's a fly buzzing about, or a stale smell in the dining room, we get out the spray can.

None of these are matters of life and death. These, and a hundred other minor inconveniences, occur to everyone all the time and are put right by easily available, inexpensive means. Now, imagine a world where you had no recourse to any means, inexpensive or otherwise, beyond what you and your family could provide for yourselves.

CONSUMPTION IN ALL ITS STAGES,

Coughs, Whooping Cough, Asthma, Bronchitis, Fever, Ague, Diphtheria, Hysteria, Rheumatism, Diarrhœa, Spasms, Colic, Renal and Uterine Diseases, are immediately relieved by a dose of

CHLORODYNE.

(Trade Mark.)

Discovered and named by DR. J. COLLIS BROWNE, M.R.C.S.L., Ex-Army Medical Staff.

The question asked by invalids, families, and households is, What is the best medicine to give in the above diseases, and what to have always ready? Medical testimony, the reply of thousands of sufferers and invalids, is confirmatory of the invaluable relief afforded by this remedy above all others.

CHLORODYNE is a liquid taken in drops according to age. It invariably relieves pain of whatever kind; creates a calm, refreshing sleep; allays irritation of the nervous system when all other remedies fail; leaving no bad effects, like opium or laudanum, and can be taken when none other can be tolerated. Its value in saving life in infancy is not easily estimated; a few drops will subdue the irritation of Teething, prevent and arrest Convulsions, cure Whooping Cough, Spasms, and Flatus at once.

Among invalids it allays the pain of Neuralgia, Rheumatism, Gout, etc. It soothes the weary achings of Consumption, relieves the Soreness of the Chest, Cough, and Expectoration; and cures all Chest Affections, such as Asthma, Bronchitis, Palpitation, etc. It checks Diarrhœa, Alvine Discharges, or Spasms, and Colics of the Intestines, etc.

The extensive demand for this remedy, known as DR. J. COLLIS BROWNE'S CHLORODYNE, by the Medical Profession, Hospitals, Dispensaries—Civil, Military, and Naval—and Families especially, guarantees that this statement of its extreme importance and value is a *bona fide* one, and worthy the attention of all.

EXTRACTS OF MEDICAL OPINIONS.

From W. VESALIUS PETTIGREW, M.D.—"I have no hesitation in stating that I have never met with any medicine so efficacious as an anti-spasmodic and sedative. I have used it in Consumption, Asthma, Diarrhœa, and other diseases, and am most perfectly satisfied with the results."

From DR. M'MILMAN, of New Galloway, Scotland.—"I consider it the most valuable medicine known."

G. HAYWARD, Esq., Surgeon, Stow-on-ye-Wold.—"I am now using Dr. J. Collis Browne's Chlorodyne with marvellous good effects in allaying inveterate sickness in pregnancy."

DR. M'GRIGOR CROFT, late Army Staff, says:—"It is a most valuable medicine."

J. C. BAKER, Esq., M.D., Bideford.—"It is without doubt the most valuable and certain anodyne we have."

DR. GIBBON, Army Medical Staff, Calcutta.—"Two doses completely cured me of Diarrhœa."

From G. V. RIDOUT, Esq., Surgeon, Egham.—"As an astringent in severe Diarrhœa, and an anti-spasmodic in Colic, with Cramps in the Abdomen, the relief is instantaneous. As a sedative in Neuralgia and Tic-Doloreux its effects were very remarkable. In Uterine Affections I have found it extremely valuable."

CAUTION.—Beware of Spurious Compounds or Imitations of "Chlorodyne." Dr. Browne placed the Recipe for making "Chlorodyne" in the hands of Mr. Davenport ONLY; consequently, there can be no other Manufacturer. The genuine bears the words, "Dr. J. Collis Browne's Chlorodyne," on the Government Stamp of each Bottle.—Sold only in Bottles at 2s. 9d., and 4s. 6d., by the Sole Agent and Manufacturer,

J. T. DAVENPORT,

33, GREAT RUSSELL STREET, BLOOMSBURY SQUARE, LONDON.

Like Lily the Pink's medicinal compound, Dr Browne's patent medicine, which he actually neglected to patent, seems to have been most efficacious in every case. Of course, in those days you didn't have to list the ingredients on the label, otherwise Doctor Browne – and all the other original inventors of the first and only true chlorodyne, such as Teasdale or Freeman – would have had to admit to opium, chloroform and cannabis, in solution in alcohol. No wonder folk thought it did them good. Eventually, publicity and legal action concerning widespread addiction and a number of fatal poisonings caused a modification of the formula.

Prodigality in the food department would never be tolerated, or even considered, in ordinary homes. If the meat was of doubtful freshness, a handful or two of the correct herbs in the pot would resolve the matter satisfactorily. Insects and smells were repelled and disguised by strewing fragrant plants about the place. You would have to make your own Ibuleve out of herbs and, probably, pig lard, and your own Elastoplast and your own Dettol. You would have to make your own diagnosis of your illness and treat it accordingly. Would you know how?

Well, if you lived in such a world and you didn't know how, you probably wouldn't last long, and such worlds are not far away historically. This writer was born in 1946, at the beginning of the age of antibiotics. Father had been brought up to believe in the powers of patent medicines: Carter's Little Liver Pills, Beecham's Powders, Beecham's Pills, Doctor J Collis Browne's Chlorodyne, Scott's Emulsion, Andrews Liver Salts, Fynnon Salt – remember Wilfred Pickles on the television, selling Fynnon Salt in that lugubrious, rumbling West Riding voice? 'Do you suffer from rheumatism, fibrositis or lumbago? Not much fun, is it.'

The writer's maternal grandmother was born in 1888, a time when Jesse Boot, son of a poor Nottinghamshire farmworker who was also the village herbalist, was making his Lobelia Pills and starting on the road to a thousand branches of Boots the Chemist, which, almost a century and a half later, are once more selling herbal remedies.

Before Jesse Boot and his pile-it-high, sell-it-cheap approach to medicines, doctors and pharmacists served only the wealthy, not that doctors knew very much anyway, and the pharmacists' remedies were mostly based in the old herbal practices and/or

FRAMPTON'S PILL OF HEALTH.

THIS excellent FAMILY PILL is a Medicine of long-tried efficacy for purifying the blood, and correcting all Disorders of the Stomach and Bowels. Two or three doses will convince the afflicted of its salutary effects. The stomach will speedily regain its strength; a healthy action of the liver, bowels, and kidneys will rapidly take place; and renewed health will be the quick result of taking this medicine, according to the directions accompanying each box.

PERSONS OF A FULL HABIT, who are subject to headache, giddiness, drowsiness, and singing in the ears, arising from too great a flow of blood to the head, should never be without them, as many dangerous symptoms will be entirely carried off by their timely use; and for elderly people, where an occasional aperient is required, nothing can be better adapted.

For FEMALES these Pills are truly excellent, removing all obstructions, the distressing headache so prevalent with the sex, depression of spirits, dulness of sight, nervous affections, blotches, pimples, and sallowness of the skin, and give a healthy juvenile bloom to the complexion.

Sold by all medicine vendors. Observe the name of "THOMAS PROUT, 229, Strand, London," on the Government Stamp. Price 1s. 1½d. and 2s 9d. per box.

BLAIR'S GOUT AND RHEUMATIC PILLS.

Price 1s. 1½d. and 2s. 9d. per box.

THIS preparation is one of the benefits which the Science of modern Chemistry has conferred upon mankind; for during the first twenty years of the present century to speak of a cure for the Gout was considered a romance; but now the efficacy and safety of this Medicine is so fully demonstrated, by unsolicited testimonials from persons in every rank of life, that public opinion proclaims this as one of the most important discoveries of the present age.

These Pills require no restraint of diet or confinement, during their use, and are certain to prevent the disease attacking any vital part.

Sold by all medicine vendors. Observe "THOMAS PROUT, 229, Strand, London," on the Government Stamp.

quackery con tricks. So, although the poor had to shift for themselves with herbs and folklore, the rich were basically getting the same thing but paying lots of dosh for it.

Going back to medieval times, if a poor person could not help herself, she went to the hospital that was run by monks or nuns who were more knowledgeable than the surrounding peasants but still had nothing beyond their herb gardens for their drug supplies.

So, what did they grow, those herb gardeners of yore, and why? Those monks and nuns mostly relied on whoever had studied and practised before and had written the knowledge down. Books were very rare, all hand-written of course, and so whatever was in them tended to be granted respect. The accepted instructive authorities were the ancient Greeks and Romans, plus a very few, slightly more recent experts such as Charlemagne, AD 747–814, King of the Franks and creator of a vast Christian empire in Western Europe.

Charlemagne spent a lot of time travelling from stronghold to stronghold, securing his military might but also encouraging the arts and sciences. Maybe he was displeased with the standard of medical care he found in the various places, or perhaps he wanted to introduce his own healthy eating programme for the citizens, but somehow he found time to make a list of the plants that should be in every garden. '*Volumus quod in horto omnes herbas habeant, id est,*' as he put it. 'We desire that, in a garden, they should have all these plants, thus.' In his own royal gardens it wasn't a question of 'should', and when it came to healthy eating, Charlemagne was a bit of a slacker. His favourite and regular dinner was a roast haunch of venison, served to him by the huntsmen who had caught the beast and not including, as far as we can tell, too many dishes of *omnes herbas*.

It's quite a list, usually counted as being of 90 herbs, food plants and fruit trees, but remember it was compiled by the emperor, a man who once had 4,500 Saxon captives put to the sword in one day at the massacre of Verden, to avenge a minor defeat at the battle of Süntelberg. Had it been a list made by the gardener, the man who had to do all the work, it might have been a great deal shorter.

The emperor's list is here given with a few notes on the more obscure (to us) of the recommended types. Because of uncertainties in translation of Charlemagne's medieval Latin, where his words have more than one possibility, both are given. Many of the same plants that we cultivate now would have been less developed in the ninth century but still recognisable to us. Celery, for instance, has the same Latin name for wild and cultivated strains, but you would find the wild so strongly flavoured as to be almost inedible, while the modern American green varieties taste almost of nothing. Charlemagne's would have been somewhere in between.

Alexanders on a misty morning in early April, growing wild on the north Norfolk coast, provides a plentiful harvest. This is 1,200 years after Charlemagne made it obligatory and 2,000 years after first plantings in Roman gardens in Britain, and the plant probably came to Britain with foreign traders before that.

Imperial Frankish Seed and Plant Catalogue, *circa* AD 800, *Carolus Maximus fecit*

Alexanders, food plant, now only seen in the wild. **Almond**. **Amaranth**, medicinal herb highly regarded by the Greeks; we grow it for decoration as love-lies-bleeding. **Angelica**, medicinal as well as edible. **Anise**, seeds used as spice and medicine, normally needs a warmer climate than ours. **Apple**. **Artemisia**, that we call southernwood, used as a sleeping draught.

Baldmoney, also called autumn gentian and bear's wort; the roots made powerful and versatile medicine. **Bay**. **Beans**, the fava/broad type and the haricot. **Beet**, probably a leafy type similar to our chards. **Burdock**, food and medicine.

Cabbages, probably several sorts, more like kale or spring greens than our delicate varieties. Another listing in the tribe we now call brassicas, **Ravacaulos** is usually given as kohl rabi but this is surely most unlikely, as this is a vegetable commonly acknowledged as developed in Germany in the 1500s. *Ravacaulos* translates roughly as 'root cabbage' or 'root (cabbage) stalk'; in French, the words are turned as *chou-rave*, 'turnip cabbage'. While it might have been an early form of kohl rabi that then disappeared, more likely it is the much older vegetable, turnip-rooted chervil. **Caper spurge**, poisonous like all the spurges, seeds used as laxative. **Caraway**. **Carrot**, or more likely **skirret**. See **pastinaca** below. **Catmint**, medicinal. **Celery**. **Centaury**, probably the wild plant *Centaurium minus*, the common centaury; medicinal (and magical). Centaury was believed to put eager folk into the right mood for witchcraft when mixed with other readily available ingredients, such as the blood of a female lapwing. Charlemagne obviously thought highly of it too.

> 'A dram of the [dried centaury] powder taken in wine, is a wonderful good help against the biting and poison of an adder. The juice of the herb with a little honey put to it, is good to clear the eyes from dimness, mists and clouds that offend or hinder sight. It is singularly good both for green and fresh wounds, as also for old ulcers and sores, to close up the one and cleanse the other, and perfectly to cure them both, although they be hollow or fistulous; the green herb, especially, being bruised and laid thereto. The decoction thereof dropped into the ears, cleanses them from worms ... and takes away all freckles, spots, and marks in the skin, being washed with it.'
>
> This is old Nick Culpeper; he also recommends it for period pains and dropsy.

Cherry, the sour and the sweet. **Chervil**. **Chestnut**. **Chickpea**. **Chicory**. **Chives**, probably a bulkier version than ours, more like a Welsh onion. **Clary sage**. **Colocynth**, also called bitter apple and bitter cucumber, a small, yellow, Turkish version of watermelon. The seeds are edible but the fruit is a violent purgative and pregnancy terminator, and it doesn't take much to overdose into fatally poisonous. **Coriander**. **Costmary**, like a mint-flavoured tansy, to which it is closely related; little grown these days although the flowers were used with lavender to perfume linen and in pot-pourri. **Cucumber**. **Cumin**. **Dictamnus**, a species of dittany native to Crete much revered medicinally. **Dill**. **Dragantea**, the dragon arum, a plant similar to our cuckoo pint, poisonous and therefore highly regarded as a purgative.

Cuckoo pint, *Arum maculatum*, aka Lords and Ladies, starchwort, every part of which is poisonous, was valued in those times when ruffs were in fashion because an excellent starch was made from its roots. While his lordship was strutting his ruff, the laundry women were suffering, 'for it chappeth, blistereth, and maketh the hands rough and rugged and withall smarting'. Portland sago, no longer available, was a kind of food-thickening agent made from this same starch.

One of the most tenacious and hated weeds of all, ground elder was once regarded as a food plant and was grown on purpose. In fact, the raw young leaves are quite pleasant to eat, with a flavour that has been lost in modern lettuce types that are grown for size and texture only.

Culpeper: 'The common use [of hazelwort] is to take the juice of five or seven leaves in a little drink to cause vomiting; the roots have also the same virtue, though they do not operate forcibly. They are very effectual against the biting of serpents, and therefore are put into Mithridate and Venice treacle.'

The treacle in question was a honey- or molasses-based antidote to venomous bites compiled by apothecaries from scores of herbal extracts. Mithridate was an earlier version said to have been invented by King Mithridates of Pontus (part of modern Turkey on the Black Sea coast), which he used to take regularly as a defence against poisoners. After many years of his own medicine, Mithridates decided to kill himself. The problem was that he had become immune, and he couldn't find a poison that did the job.

Endive. Fennel. Fenugreek. Fig. Garlic. Gourd. Goutweed, also known as bishop's weed, herb Gerard, pigweed, medicinal against gout and sciatica, was also a food plant. Modern gardeners will be shocked that Charlemagne commended this plant to be grown on purpose. We know it most familiarly as ground elder. **Hazel. Hazelwort**, properly asarabacca, medicinal, found wild in northern uplands.

Heliotrope, slightly poisonous, no medicinal value so presumably grown for its fragrance. **Houseleek**, *Sempervivum tectorum*, in Latin the plant that lives for ever on roofs, had many medicinal uses but Charlemagne reputedly had its protective reputation in mind. Houses on which it grew were said to be proof against fire, thunderstorms and witchcraft. **Juniper. Leek. Lettuces**, several sorts. Charlemagne would have known the cos type and the curly, pick-as-you-go ones, plus the ancestor wild lettuce that produced a mild narcotic and sedative in its plentiful juice. **Lilies**, called by Charlemagne *lilium* and *gladiolum*. The latter in Latin is 'sword lily', probably meaning flag iris here. The lilies could have been both the white madonna and the red martagon types, with many medicinal uses, and the bulbs were cooked to make a sweet, soothing dish. **Lovage**.

Madder, plants for making dyes. **Marsh mallow**, the young leaves of which made a fine salad and the roots thereof a delicate dish fried in butter, and **Tree mallow**. Mallows had a reputation as health givers, curers of all ills, possibly because of their purgative effect. **Medlar. Melon**; Charlemagne's word *pepones* can also mean pumpkins, but as we already have gourds, it probably is melons.

Mints, *mentastrum* (wild mint) and *menta* (garden mint). **Mulberry. Mustard**, probably the one we call white mustard, which we sow traditionally with cress for a quick salad and which gives a milder condiment from its seeds.

Onion. Orach, or arrach, or mountain spinach, related to fat hen and good king Henry. **Parsley. Pastinaca**, usually translated as parsnip although in Latin it also meant carrot, the Romans having a root vegetable somewhere between the two. **Pea**, but not the garden pea we grow, which was developed in Renaissance Italy. This was the field pea, something like the one we call carlin, to be dried and long cooked, regarded as peasant or animal food. **Peach. Pear**.

Pennyroyal, the smallest and most aromatic of the mints, *Mentha pulegium*, was one of the most revered herbs in ancient times. Its virtues were such that warm ashes of the burnt plant could revive flies and bees that had previously been put to drown, which demonstration would have been enough to convince anyone of the integrity of the demonstrator. Quite how that works with the plant's fame as an insect repellent – the Romans called it *puleium*, fleabane – is not clear. **Pine**, the stone pine, is the one that gives us pine nuts. **Plum. Poppy**, surely not the red one with such limited use confined to its seeds in bread baking and oil making. Much more likely it was the white one, the opium poppy, source of the best natural sedative and painkiller known in ancient times – and modern times, come to that.

Quince. Radish. Rocket. Roman coriander, *Nigella sativa*, also called flower fennel, is neither coriander nor fennel but a buttercup. The seeds, now called black cumin and *quatre épices*, were the useful part, in the kitchen, called in Latin, would you believe, *git*. **Roses**. **Rosemary**. **Rue.**

Sage. **Savory**, not clear if winter or summer, or both. **Service tree**. **Seseli**, similar to cow parsley, also called moon carrot and stone parsley, from which we have the name sweet cicely. **Shallot**. **Squill**, the bulbs of which are dried and powdered and used for many medicinal purposes. Readers of a certain age may have taken it in the original formulation of Gee's Linctus. Like so many of these natural remedies, too much is poisonous.

Tansy. **Teasel,** used in cloth making. **Thyme,** in Charlemagne's list *sisymbrium*, sometimes given as water mint but much more likely to be thyme, which is not mentioned otherwise and was a plant sacred to Venus, as was that called *sisymbrium* by the Romans. **Walnut**. **Watercress.**

'Consider the lilies of the field, how they grow; they toil not, neither do they spin: And yet I say unto you, that even Solomon in all his glory was not arrayed like one of these' (Matthew 6:28). Scholars tend to identify the lily in question as the purple martagon or Turk's cap. Possibly those tillers in holy orders, who did so much for garden plants in the medieval monasteries and hospitals, would have seen the same truth in something as humble as the wild stitchwort.

So, there you have it: the list of plants you must grow. Not stated is all the mumbo-jumbo that went with every single thing on that list. The Roman writers, such as Cato, used to mix empirically observed truth with folklore and religion and call it science, in Cato's case De Re Rustica, 'Of Things Rural', and people of Charlemagne's era would have believed the lot. Even today you will easily find gardeners who will tell you to plant only in certain phases of the moon, or to point your seeds to the east, or something, and in between times the magic and mystery were held to be essential to success.

When is a herb not a herb? Birdsfoot trefoil, *Lotus corniculatus*, has no herbal tradition in Europe. You can't eat it, as you'd be ingesting hydrogen cyanide and sometimes prussic acid. Small quantities of hydrogen cyanide will improve digestion and encourage breathing, which is why the plant features in old Chinese herbal medicine texts, but larger quantities tend to stop breathing altogether. All its poisons disappear when the plant is dried.

Because of its looks, it has about seventy different names, including bacon and eggs, lady's slipper and granny's toenails, and the bees like it. It's being encouraged as a forage plant in America, where tests have shown that milk from cows fed on trefoil hay is especially high in vitamins A and E. According to the Department of Plant Science at McGill University, Canada, the birdsfoot trefoil is particularly suitable for use in 'genetic manipulation strategies' and, indeed, it has been 'clonally micropropagated'. And you can't say fairer than that.

So much so, in fact, that we have had an example of the genetic modification of tannin biosynthesis in birdsfoot trefoil for the introduction of a heterologous dihydroflavonol reductase gene into hairy root cultures. So maybe it is a herb after all.

Salsa verde, *circa* AD 1400

The modern Italian version may feature parsley, garlic, gherkins, capers, lemon juice and anchovy fillets, all ingredients available from the shops, but the medieval original is much more challenging. It contains no fish, its prime purpose being to disguise the taste of fish which, the recipe writer predicted, might be slightly off.

You need 'percely, myntes, diteyne, peletre and cost marye' to start with. 'Diteyne' is the false or white dittany we call burning bush. The name 'peletre', or pellitory, usually refers to the pellitory of Spain, *Anacyclus pyrethrum*, something like chamomile to look at, cultivated for its pungent root as a remedy for toothache so not likely to go in a sauce. Sneezewort, *Achillea ptarmica*, was also called pellitory but that doesn't seem very likely either; it and its relative yarrow were once grown for medicinal purposes but are hardly good sources of green stuff. So, the vote goes to pellitory-of-the-wall, *Parietaria officinalis*, a close relative of the stinging nettle and a native of this country, which at least has pick-worthy leaves.

Anyway, with your parsley, mint, costmary and burning bush if you can get them, and probably some young nettles instead of pellitory, add white bread which has been soaked in vinegar, and plenty of pepper. Mix it all up, adding more vinegar if necessary, or 'eisel'. Eisel is sometimes just another word for vinegar or, more particularly, a condiment made by steeping the leaves of wormwood and other herbs in wine, presumably not the best wine. It is possible this cook was just referring to two sorts of vinegar, as we might with malt and cider, say.

If you do make this and want to serve it to guests, consider having some of the conventional Italian version too, as back up.

Medieval herb salad

This is from *The Boke of Nurture* written by Bishop John Russell around 1460. The good bishop was an important minister under Edward IV and, amazingly in those Roses days of axe and block for erring high risers, he was chancellor to both Yorkist Richard III and Lancastrian Henry VII. Anyone who could keep his head thus, when all around were losing theirs, and be Bishop of Lincoln while at it, must surely be respected as one who knew his onions.

'*Salat: Take parsel, sawge, garlec, chibollas* [ciboule, Welsh onion]*, oynons, leek, borage, myntes, porrectes* [another word for leek or onion, probably means more of another sort of onion – or leek]*, fenel, and ton tressis* [watercress]*, rew, rosemarye, purslayne,* *lave, and waisshe hem clene* ['lave' just means wash, so double wash them clean]. *Pike hem, pluk hem small with thyn hond* [pick over them and tear or slice them] *and myng hem well with rawe oil. Lay on vynegar and salt and serve it forth.'*

When mynging your salad, you could use lemon juice instead of vinegar. For rawe oil, the Bishop would have used olive. You could leave out the rue for a less assertive flavour.

Much of the development of horticulture came through the monks and nuns working in abbeys, monasteries and hospitals, studying the best ways to improve food plants and medicinal herbs to the great benefit of everyone. A German monk of the ninth century called Walafrid Strabo (Walafrid with the Squint, poor man), a contemporary of Charlemagne, wrote a poem, '*Hortulus*', 'Little Garden', in which he describes making raised beds and lists his most valued plants. His herb list isn't all that different from the imperial one: sage and rue come first in prestige; the rest would mostly be familiar to educated gardeners of the time and to those who scoured the hedgerows and waysides for medicines: agrimony, betony, catmint, celery, chervil, clary, horehound, fennel, iris, lily, lovage, mint, pennyroyal, poppy, rose, southernwood, tansy, wormwood.

Another poem, '*The Feate of Gardening*', published by Master John the Gardener around the middle of the fifteenth century, adds to Charlemagne's and the Squinter's lists with borage, bugle, foxglove, herb robert, hollyhock, lavender (surely the most surprising omission so far), marigold, mullein, pimpernel, ragged robin, St John's wort, scabious, valerian, violet, viper's bugloss and woodruff. Some authorities give marigold as corn marigold, for which farmers would not have thanked Master John. It's a most invasive weed in cereal crops which, like ragwort in hay meadows, was the equivalent of a notifiable disease. Nor is it clear why he would recommend it, unless it was for its looks. Much more likely it was the one we call pot marigold, calendula, a most useful herb for salads and for skin ailments.

Another unable to resist the poetic muse was Thomas Tusser, scholar, court musician and East Anglian farmer, who versified his *Hundreth Good Pointes of Husbandrie* in 1557, later enlarged to include an additional *Hundreth Good Pointes of Huswifery* and, after many printings, to *Five Hundreth Good Pointes of Husbandrie*.

The first proper gardening book in English prose was written by Thomas Hyll, who was born around 1528. It had a very snappy title: *A most briefe and pleasaunt treatyse, teachynge howe to dress, sowe, and set a garden, and what propertyes also these few herbes heare spoken of, have to our comodytie: with the remedyes that may be used against such beasts, wormes, flies and such lyke, that commonly noy gardens, gathered out of the principallest authors in this act by Thomas Hyll, Londyner, 1563.*

Hyll died before he had completed his revised and improved edition, published in

1577 as *The Gardeners Labyrinth*. In it he added strawberry, asparagus, spinach as a plant separate from orach, and artichoke to the fruit and veg section, and for herbs he introduced blessed thistle, or holy thistle, a heal-all import from southern Europe, and buck's horn, a native type of plantain with small, divided leaves that likes the seaside.

Also in 1577 William Harrison, a collaborator in *Holinshed's Chronicles*, described how the cultivation of vegetables and herbs, latterly fallen into disuse and disarray in England through times of civil war, religious strife and pestilence, had at last begun to recover.

> *Great thanks therefore be given unto the physicians of our age and country, who not only endeavour to search out the use of such simples as our soil doth yield and bring forth, but also to procure such as grow elsewhere, upon purpose so to acquaint them with our clime that they in time, through some alteration received from the nature of the earth, may likewise turn to our benefit and commodity and be used as our own.*

Where comfrey gets a hold, it certainly can be prolific. A free green vegetable for 'country folk' and a cure-all for everyone, especially of inward hurts and outward wounds, dear old Culpeper recommended it for broken bones, the roots being so powerful 'that if they be boiled with dissevered pieces of flesh in a pot, it will join them together again'.

Coming later and bigger than cow parsley, hemlock is easily distinguished by its spotted, hairless stem. It was the favoured poison of the ancient Greek judicial system and of English romantic poets – 'My heart aches, and a drowsy numbness pains/My sense, as though of hemlock I had drunk' ('Ode to a Nightingale', John Keats) – and it has been used in medicine since earliest times, although it has lost its reputation of late. According to Mrs Grieve, this is 'owing to the uncertain action of the preparations made from it'.

Cow parsley is the closest relative in the wild of chervil, and is not so dissimilar in culinary potential, especially when young, as here. Perhaps because it is so common it has tended to be dismissed but it really is a valuable flavouring and salading, and not only for rabbits. Of course it must not be confused with fool's parsley, a spindly, smaller, hairless, weedier specimen, but poisonous, and above all not with hemlock.

Chapter Two

Perennial Herbs

The chief dividers of herbs from the cultivator's point of view are our climate and the means of propagation. Some herbs are perennials in this country, and some self-seed so efficiently that they may as well be perennial. Some are naturally perennials but are tender and so must be treated and sown as annuals here. Some are biennials, but their usefulness is in their first year and so are best sown each year anyway.

Of course, hardly anyone will want to grow all of the plants in this book. Not even a herb nursery would be likely to stock them all, yet this long list is nowhere near as long as it could be. Besides usefulness and beauty and disallowing those requiring too much palaver in the growing, the main criterion for inclusion has been frequency of mention in the older and classical books.

As with all forms of horticulture, herb gardening is a blend of art and science, and you are never going to find all the artists and scientists agreeing on every point, so this list is, in effect, a kind of opinion poll among the eminent herbers of the past, all of whom have gone to the great herb garden in the sky and so cannot be consulted. This writer can only hope that they approve.

So, let us look first at the hardy perennials, the ones that, once away, need little interference from you until they need replacing through old age (theirs, not yours). These are largely the cultivated culinary and floral plants which also have a medicinal tradition, and the wild ones that manage themselves in nature but will need some management in the garden. Seeds of a great many wild herbs, previously only available by *in situ* gathering and friendly gifts, can now be obtained easily and at low cost from a number of specialised growers.

For the powers, real and imagined, of the more obscure medicinal plants, you should consult one of the encyclopaedic herbals, such as Mrs Grieve's.

Some of the culinary ones are flavourings, some salads, some vegetables to be cooked, and some are not so much to shout about on their own but have been, in that traditional phrasing, useful in soups. This does not imply that, in the olden days when foodstuffs were hunted and gathered free by knowledgeable four-year-olds, mother made soup as a first course to precede the sole Colbert, roast partridge and lemon meringue pie. Poorer families had one pot and one kettle to go on the fire and dinner generally consisted of whatever could be got in season, all put in the one pot to make a pottage, and that could include anything from the roots of avens to the leaves of ground elder to the flowers of the lesser knapweed and back again.

Perhaps the greatest novelty for modern herb gardeners is the marvellous variety suddenly available in salads. This writer's mother's idea of salad was lettuce, tomato, cucumber and hard-boiled egg, and she never varied it in the slightest degree. Next door did something similar but without the hard-boiled egg and with the addition of raw onion, and all of it soaked, really soaked, in malt vinegar (we had Heinz Salad Cream). Now, with a herb garden, the combinations of leaves and flowers are almost infinite in their possibilities. Your correspondent can still remember, many years ago, the first time he added sorrel and lemon balm to some shredded lettuce. It was a revelation. So, let's to it.

Angelica, *Angelica archangelica*

The wild kind native to Britain, *Angelica sylvestris*, likes damp conditions and the combination of light and shade you find in a clearing in the forest. It has reddish/purplish stems, with its white flowers tinged with the colour supposedly of Bordeaux wine. It's a member of the *Umbelliferae* tribe, like hemlock, cow parsley, fool's parsley, giant hogweed and so on, requiring care and accuracy in identification. It can grow to four or five feet and is more bitter and less rewarding as a herb than the larger, fatter, more aromatic, cultivated, garden species, *A. archangelica/officinalis*, which has greenish stems, darker and purple-tinted at the base, and yellow-green flowers. This also has become naturalised in many regions so as to be more common in the wild than its native relation.

Once indispensible to cake decorators, and of equal standing to cherries with mothers who made iced buns, angelica has almost disappeared from view. Even in its heyday, few of those who used the sticky little green fragments of stem would have recognised this plant as the source.

The most frequent and traditional use is of the stems, candied, to be deployed in fancy confectionery, but this has declined greatly as artificial products have become more easily available. Candying is a laborious process and modern tastes, used to the exotica of the world, conclude that it is hardly worth the bother.

In colder parts of the world where angelica is happy to flourish, such as Iceland, northern Germany and Scandinavia, the whole plant is treated as a vegetable. In warmer climes, where the grape is king, the seeds are important in the secret recipes for certain vermouths and liqueurs. In Britain, where rhubarb is plentiful in the spring, persons normally reluctant to eat the pink stuff can be persuaded sometimes by the addition of angelica stems to the pan.

In earlier times, angelica was revered for its medicinal properties, in particular as a means of repelling infection. It was alleged to be a power against the plague. Those folk living in large towns in the summer, when all manner of diseases were floating about, were advised to keep a stem of angelica always in the mouth, like chewing gum. If any witches or evil spirits were likewise hovering in wait, angelica would keep them away too. A decoction of the root mixed with honey, lemon and brandy was used to treat typhus.

Modern herbalists recommend a tea made from the leaves as a great tonic, especially when taken regularly for some days, which seems a good deal cheaper and more likely to work than some similar programmes advertised on the television. 'Take the angelica leaf-tea challenge!' will not make the tills ring, however.

It's a big plant and not strictly a perennial since it dies after seeding, maybe in its third year, which can of course be prevented by removing the flower heads before they ripen, giving a longer-living plant. Seeding will generally produce more than enough new plants, but the seeds do not keep. Large plants, which spread without encouragement, need placing carefully in the garden and, although angelica likes moisture and part shade, it will forgive you for not providing a babbling woodland brook to grow by.

Avens, or herb bennet, *Geum urbanum*

Now that mothballs are illegal, perhaps there will be a revival in the cultivation of this modest little plant, the slowly dried roots of which were used to keep moths away. They were also said to keep Satan away from your house but no reliable evidence for their effectiveness in this task can be found. The roots smell of cloves and are chewed, fresh, to sweeten the breath, and are UiS (Useful in Soups).

In the wild, avens likes damp and not too much sun so, in mid and late summer, its small yellow flowers will tend to appear in woods and shady lanes. The flowers turn into dark red burrs, which attach themselves to passing rabbits and to you, should you

Were you to wear a bracelet made of this herb, you could be sure of not encountering any evil spirits or venomous beasts, and even the very devil himself would fly from you. You can easily prove this yourself. Its modern name, herb bennet, is a contraction of the Latin *herba benedicta*, the herb which is blessed, and it has been closely connected to the Christian church in many ways although the belief in its powers probably goes back further. Its other proper name, avens, may be linked to the ancient Sanskrit root of verbs of wishing and loving.

wish to grow avens in your garden, or you can buy seeds from wildflower sources, a quid for a thousand. The roots are dug up in March according to tradition, when they are at their most pungent.

Balm, or lemon balm, *Melissa officinalis*

Culinarily, as chives are to onions so balm is to lemon. In salads, in teas, as a flavouring with eggs and fish, it has a hundred uses and will grow well enough to supply them. Although it slightly prefers to have its feet damp, balm will grow anywhere. One plant from the village fete will see you right in balm for all of your days, and you will soon be pulling it up and telling it to behave itself.

It was considered an important medicinal herb, mainly for its cheering effect, and was often prescribed steeped in wine. Possibly the wine helped with the cheering. It was also used to heal wounds: the juice being squeezed from the leaves and applied as a styptic

To make a really excellent bed for a prawn cocktail, take the whole leaves of lettuce thinnings and mix with the torn leaves of lemon balm. This is approximately one hundred times better than sliced iceberg. Lemon balm, the cheerful herb, is also excellent in salads, egg mayo sandwiches, and egg mayo salad sandwiches.

and antiseptic – a practice which seems to have its basis in scientific fact. Not quite so scientific was *The London Dispensary* of 1696, which stated that 'essence of balm, given in Canary wine every morning, will renew youth, strengthen the brain, relieve languishing nature and prevent baldness'.

Here, then, is a message for young, long-haired male poets everywhere. Instead of languishing all over the place and wasting your time composing verses to your love until your hair falls out, strengthen your brain with some lemon balm from the allotment.

It is generally recommended that you pick the leaves before the plant flowers. Curiously, it being such a merry maker, balm is also prescribed for insomniacs and those of a nervous disposition.

Bergamot, or bee balm, *Monarda didyma*

Nothing to do with the bergamot orange, the oil of which is used to flavour Earl Grey tea, this herb nevertheless has a scent reminiscent of the said Earl's favourite beverage and many other fine qualities also. It is quite showy enough for a border, with its scarlet flowers, and it grows eagerly. Bees love it.

For preference, give it part shade and fairly moist ground; its wild home is in America beside water, for instance the River Oswego in New York State from which it gets its American common name, Oswego tea. Such a beverage is made from the young leaves. Another American is *M. fistulosa*, which they call wild bergamot, a medicinal herb of the native tribes right across what is now the USA, growing in woodlands.

Betony, or bishopswort, *Stachys betonica*

Betony belongs with the dead-nettle family and looks like it, though with showier, purple-red flowers later in the season than the white and the red of that ilk. Unlike them, it has a rather bitter taste and so is not much use in the kitchen.

It is often grown for ornament only, and for its special attraction to bees, and cultivation is as easy as with any nettle or mint. Perhaps such growers are unaware of its medical

With one of the biggest reputations among the ancients, betony of all herbs was offered as a cure-all for physical and mental ailments. It was associated closely with headaches and the workings of the brain, and was supposed to protect against bad dreams and other unpleasant visions.

reputation, it being extolled as a certain remedy for between thirty and fifty diseases, depending on which ancient physician you believe. For these purposes, the whole plant is dried and crumbled; a drink quite like tea can be made from this, or it can be put in a roll-up and smoked to relieve headache, or taken as snuff for the same reason. In the eighteenth century, when there was something of a vogue for green snuffs, that is snuffs made from herbs rather than tobacco, betony was a key ingredient, partly because of belief in it as a head-clearer and partly because it was a near-infallible sneeze inducer. Mixed with honey and vinegar 'it helpeth those that spit blood, and is good for those that have a rupture and are bruised'. If you have no headache nor rupture, you can still get a splinter while gardening, in which case you can try rubbing the green leaves on the affected part to help draw the splinter out.

Bistort, *Polygonum bistorta*

Twice twisted, the name means, and that refers to the rhizome, which is a powerful astringent/styptic once used in tanning leather. Like all of the *Polygonum* clan, which are

The cultivated version of bistort is *Polygonum bistorta superbum*. A scientific experiment under laboratory conditions revealed that eight out of ten people thought that was SUperbum, as in Superman, and not suPERbum as in superb which, of course, is what it is, and that only goes to show what kind of minds most people have. Superbum is much more showy and precise in its poker heads than the wild type.

the knotweeds, it bears large numbers of small, bell-shaped flowers, pink in this case.

Whether the leaves of *superbum* are as good in dock pudding must be decided in northern England. The wild one, unhappy in the effete south, only thrives in the rough, tough north, specifically in Cumbria and in the Calder valley in the Yorkshire Pennines, where they even go so far as to have a World Dock Pudding Championship. The docks in question are the leaves of the bistort, gathered from the moors and cooked with onions, nettles, oatmeal, butter and seasoning. The resulting green mess is served with egg, bacon and potato cake.

Regular ingestion of dock pudding may be responsible for the low incidence of piles among the good folk of Mytholmroyd, if indeed there is a low incidence, such are the curative properties ascribed to bistort by the old herbalists.

Borage, *Borago officinalis*

Cultivated for its fine appearance in flower, its possibilities as a vegetable and for its traditional use in gladdening hearts and dispelling melancholy, borage is often found in the wild as a garden escape, on poor, dry ground. This it likes, so gardeners should avoid giving it much care and attention. It's a big plant too, and will seed itself and spread with no assistance.

The flowers are brilliant blue stars with a blue-black cone in the centre; leaves, as with its close relatives bugloss and comfrey, are hairy. It is by no means alone among herbs in being praised for its ability, when mixed with wine, to make people merry, although it would demand a controlled experiment with boraged and unboraged wine to ascertain the actual degree of merriment due to the plant. Should too much merriment ensue, resulting in a fogginess of mind, boiling water should be poured on to the fresh or dried leaves and the steam inhaled. Certainly a salad with the cucumber-ish leaves and the spectacular flowers is enough to gladden anyone's heart.

In days of old in every school, even the most youthful pupils would have had no trouble in translating this maxim: *Ego borago gaudia semper ago.* 'I, borage, inner gladness always I put in motion,' which might have had the Latin master suggesting a slightly more free translation, for example, 'I, borage, bring you joy, every time a coconut.'

You would hardly believe the many abilities of the
humble bracken, *Pteris aquiline*, feather of the
eagle. It's one of the commonest plants and
regarded in a low light, yet, if you knew certain
secrets about it, you would surely amaze your
neighbours by growing it in your herb garden.
Why? Because it can render you invisible, it can
grant you eternal youth, it can kill both the broad
and the long worms in your body, and it can stop
your barrels of wine going off. The latter two
virtues use the root, the former use the seed.
Bracken seed is similar in some respects to hen's
teeth and unicorn droppings, so youthful
invisibility must remain a promise unfulfilled until
further research can be conducted.

The flower of the bluebell, *Endymion nonscriptus*, has no use at all beyond its
breathtaking beauty in numbers. The bulb, which is poisonous, was used as a styptic
and as the raw material for a starchy glue – minor uses that are now forbidden as the
plant is protected. Although it grows in a number of European countries, something
like three quarters of all wild bluebells grow in the British Isles.

Burning bush, *Dictamnus albus*

Another showy plant with a fine fragrance, this is a herb with a unique feature. That lemony smell comes from an oil that vapourises on a hot, dry, windless day and, if you catch it just right, at eventide, and when the plant has lots of older flower heads, you can put a flame near the plant and ignite a small and harmless conflagration.

The root has minor medicinal properties which are now out of favour; the leaves, yet again, make a tea of sorts.

Catmint, *Nepeta cataria*

Quite a versatile mint, it used mainly to be grown for its tea-making qualities, offering the savour and stimulation of a cup of China without the expense. Chewing the root offers even more stimulation, apparently, since the admirable Frances Bardswell relates a story of a hangman who never could screw up the courage to pull the handle until he'd had a good old chew of catmint.

The blue flowers are pretty too, and many medicinal uses are listed. As is often the case, the old doctors found so many virtues in the plant that one begins to wonder why anybody bothered to grow anything else. Apart from being of use in fever, insomnia, colic and insanity, bruises, smallpox, piles and scarlet fever, you can also make a jam of the young floral tops which is 'serviceable for nightmare'.

Be warned, however. The name is no folklore. Cats will walk a mile for catmint and will writhe and wriggle among it until it is destroyed. So, if you would like your garden to be a magnet for cats, you have the answer. On the other hand, it is said to repel rats.

Chamomile, *Anthemis nobilis*

The famous chamomile lawn, once a usual feature of grand houses and royal palaces, was so popular not only for its fragrance and beauty, and because it stayed green in the driest weather, but also because really good grass seed wasn't so easy to come by. While the rich man in his castle had it because it was bright and beautiful, and because he and his lady liked to stroll on chamomile paths and rest on chamomile-covered seats, the poor man at his gate also grew the herb, partly as a general-purpose medicine for himself and partly because it was a doctor plant, supposed to ensure the health of all plants growing near it.

It doesn't taste as nice as it smells. The apple-ish fragrance gives way to a very bitter flavour, but the dried flowers make – of course – a tea, and this is acknowledged to be a quietener of jangled nerves and a settler of upset stomachs, either drunk in the normal way or the steam of it inhaled. Indeed, some authorities go further and suggest it to be an 'extremely efficacious remedy for hysterical and nervous affections in women', but your correspondent cannot vouch for this, never having wanted to cure a woman of affections, nervous or otherwise. Other authorities caution against excessive chamomile use, in case dizziness results.

The Cultivation of Chamomile Lawns.

The chamomiles generally used for lawns are the single and double varieties of ANTHEMIS NOBILIS, both of which are close growing and soon form a compact mat of finely cut aromatic foliage of a delightful bright green. Both give off a delicious scent when trodden upon or on a warm summer evening after rain.

The ground should be well forked over a little time before planting and some leaf soil or some other clean organic compost may be mixed in the surface or dug in. It is very important that the bed should be free of weeds or weed seeds so as to give the small plants a chance to establish themselves and start to spread before weeds have time to spring up and smother them.

Chamomile plants are best planted in April or May - allow six inches each way and make the soil firm round the roots, Once established the plants will soon send out runners and fill in the intervening spaces. Unless the lawn has grown exceptionally well as it may do in a wet summer, it is advisable to allow it to grow freely without mowing for the first season. Cut off the straggling flower grown in the autumn, top dress with good fine soil and the lawn will be ready for mowing in the following spring but NOT before April or May.

Another method of making a chamomile lawn is to sow seed of the single variety - the double variety does not seed - on a finely prepared bed of soil made ready as if for the sowing of a grass lawn. Sow evenly and cover with a fine dressing of sieved soil. Keep very free of weeds as the chamomile seedlings are very easily smothered before they have a chance to develop. Once established the sown lawn should receive the same treatment as a lawn formed of plants but it should not be walked on or mown until the plants have formed a mat of roots and foliage. Chamomile does NOT like lime.

We strongly recommend the DOUBLE variety as being by far the most satisfactory in appearance and durability.

Various creeping thymes can be introduced into a lawn for variety, and also creeping pennyroyal which is also excellent for pathways or paving. "The Judges Choice" catalogue will give you details of all these and prices. We will also design gardens for you for a very moderate fee, or put you in touch with a firm of landscape gardeners who specialse in the arrangement of herb gardens. At all times we are at your service for advice.

With the compliments of MURRAY ELLIS LTD.
Herb Farm Produce,
BRIDPORT, Dorset. phone 2096.

The flowers should be gathered as soon as possible after the third flowering day, if they are to be used medicinally, and dried in an airy place that isn't too hot. There are various other chamomiles besides the true, including German, stinking, corn and yellow. The Spanish call the true chamomile *manzanilla* but do not, as told elsewhere, use it to flavour the sherry of that name. Rather, the slightly bitter taste of the sherry is reminiscent to those Spaniards of chamomile tea and so is called after it.

To make the tea by the traditional method: put about thirty flowers into a jug, pour a pint of boiling water upon them, cover up the tea, and when it has stood about ten minutes, pour it off from the flowers into another jug; sweeten with sugar or honey; drink a teacupful of it, fasting in the morning to strengthen the digestive organs and restore the liver to healthier action. A teacupful of chamomile tea, in which is stirred a large dessert-spoonful of moist sugar and a little grated ginger, is an excellent thing to administer to aged people a couple of hours before their dinner.

Chicory, or succory, *Cichorium intybus*

The Latin name is two words meaning the same thing, so this is the perennial 'chicory chicory', as opposed to *Cichorium endivia*, chicory endive, which is a half-hardy annual. With your hardy perennial chicory, rather than go through all that time-consuming business of blanching just to get a bit of fancy salad out of season, let it grow and you will have an eight-feet high, blue-flowered glory that will give you a show right through the late summer and into the autumn. Bees like it, although they have to work in the mornings because, sunshine or no, the chicory-chicory clock knows when it's lunchtime and closes up its flowers for the day.

The medicinal uses are all in the root, which is also used to make a kind of coffee. The young leaves are fine in a plain salad although rather bitter on their own.

Chives, *Allium schoenoprasum*

Everybody knows what chives are and how to use them. They have no medicinal tradition. You can cut and come again as often as the plant will stand it and if you allow it to seed you will have chives all over the place. Chives will not dry; you have to freeze it if you want to keep some for winter, when the plant disappears entirely.

Comfrey, *Symphytum officinale*

This is a big, rough, hairy version of borage, historically valued for all sorts of reasons but chiefly now grown for its qualities as a compost ingredient and fertiliser, especially good for potatoes and tomatoes. Seed potatoes set on a layer of comfrey leaves will greatly benefit, and tomatoes like a liquid feed made with comfrey leaves torn up and

About thirty years before the time of writing, your correspondent had a Damascene experience concerning egg sandwiches. Experience of that comestible had been limited, and had convinced him that the only thing worse than an egg sandwich was an egg and tomato sandwich. Moving to the country, the new next door neighbour was a lady called Eileen and, one lunchtime, she offered egg sandwiches. These were assembled from her homemade, wholemeal bread, which was like cake, eggs from her runabout, scratchabout hens, homemade mayonnaise and chives. Chives had not been noticed before, possibly not even seen before, not even in upmarket London restaurants. If an egg sandwich with a herb can change a life, Eileen's did just that. Some years later, your correspondent's own Madame made egg sandwiches for the cricket tea. The home team's opening bowler complained that someone had put grass in his.

Here in a Suffolk wood in late April, comfrey is just preparing to come into flower while its companion, alexanders, is much further on in its annual cycle.

left in water for a week. Cultivated, developed varieties such as Bocking No 4 are better to eat than the original wild type. All sorts like partial shade and are indifferent to the ground they grow in, although will flourish if better looked after.

Comfrey leaves were always thought to be excellent wound and bruise healers and, by extension, a decoction thereof was thought to be good for internal wounds such as piles and ulcers. The leaves were also credited with beneficial influence on the knitting of broken bones, possibly because they tend to take the swelling down. The root is said to have similar attributes but more so. An old recipe puts a quarter pound of thinly sliced comfrey root in boiling water for ten or fifteen minutes. The resulting strained liquor should be used for soaking bandages, which are then placed as a poultice on injured joints.

Costmary, or alecost, *Tanacetum balsamita*

A more aromatic and better tasting, slightly minty version of our wild tansy, costmary is an Asian import of long ago, very commonly grown in country gardens. It likes full sun and is UK-hardy but will very rarely seed in this country, so the stock must be multiplied by division. In shade it probably won't flower either, denying those who wish to imitate their ancestral grandmothers who would put costmary flowers with lavender in their linen presses. In the wardrobe or wherever they kept their woollies, costmary's insect-repellent qualities would help to keep the moths off.

The name 'alecost' is usually enough evidence for a statement along the lines of 'used to flavour beer in the old days before hops'. Hops have been used in brewing in this country since Saxon times and costmary only arrived *circa* 1500, so the truth is more likely connected with hops' fussiness about where they grow and costmary/alecost's more carefree attitude. Alecost gives a spicy rather than bitter flavour and does not offer the full range of hop attributes and actions in the brewing process so, as brewing changed from a home-based to an almost entirely commercial activity, the superior hop replaced the other herb.

Costmary was also supposed to be used in mulled wines, particularly the one associated with royal horseman Colonel Negus, although how it held its flavoursome own against the powers of port, cloves, nutmeg and lemon we cannot tell without a recipe. Possibly it was used where more expensive spices could not be afforded.

Other costmary qualities are as a flavouring herb in cooking, and as a salading, and it had well-acknowledged but minor medicinal uses as a stomach settler and laxative. Beyond that, we find among the ancients an embracing enthusiasm for such a plethora of virtues that we cannot help but be amazed and wonder who did the research.

The juice expressed from the leaves was, according to one authority, good for the shakes and was to be recommended to those who 'are apt to have the gout fly upwards into the stomach'. Earlier practitioners made a preserve of the leaves with sugar, which 'doth warm and dry the braine and openeth the stoppings of the same'. And you didn't need much of your costmary jam. The 'quantitie of a beane' would open your brain stoppings and, moreover, clear your catarrh, 'rheumes and all distillations'.

An eighteenth-century writer says the juice of the herb was good in cases of quotidian ague, which was the name given to any kind of acute fever, malarial or otherwise, of which the symptoms returned daily. One has to assume that it didn't really work too well, because it was later superceded by treatments including arsenic by mouth and quinine by rectum.

Creeping Jenny, or moneywort, *Lysimachia nummularia*

Herb twopence, they used to call it, because its pairs of round leaves on the ground looked a little like pennies. Every garden used to have it, mainly because of its value against cuts and bruises, but partly because it will grow in an unfavourable, damp and dark spot and brighten that up with its golden flowers.

The fruit of the dogwood, or dogberry, *Cornus sanguinea*, was supposed to make a cure for rabies in people and the bark an anti-mange bath for dogs, although in rabies it's a rather desperate measure as the berries are mildly poisonous. Flower and fruit-bearing twigs are deep red, hence the name sanguinea, bloody. Quite why Shakespeare chose Dogberry as the name of his comic constable in *Much Ado* is not known, but we can guess that he just liked it. The mature wood of the shrub is remarkably hard and is traditionally used for those parts of a wooden construction taking the most punishment, such as the rungs of ladders, and there are many fancy varieties for the garden which are prized for flowers, berries and brightly coloured bark.

One of the names of elecampane, or wild sunflower, is horseheal, which is testament to one of its qualities. It has many human uses too. Nicholas Culpeper says that the root should be 'boiled well in vinegar, beaten afterwards and made into an ointment with hog's suet or oil of trotters'. This unguent of delight will prove 'a most excellent remedy for scabs or itch in young and old'. Although Master Culpeper is often wide of the mark, here his commendations have some merit, because the root of elecampane does contain a bactericide.

Elecampane, *Inula helenium*

Also called wild sunflower and scabwort, it is widespread but rare in the wild in the UK, though elecampane has been cultivated for thousands of years because its root had many uses. To post-banquet Romans it was the equivalent of Rennies or Milk of Magnesia, with added cheer-up. The Anglo-Saxons appreciated it too, as a general cure for chesty complaints and as a veterinary medicine. The name 'scabwort' may come from its use on animals with skin diseases, saddle sores and so on.

The root has also been used in cooking. The Romans made a sharp sauce with it and in England there used to be a sweetmeat which acted as a digestif, supposedly the candied root although latterly it had as much to do with the original as marshmallows now have with theirs.

It is a big plant, one of the so-called 'stately herbs', liking shade and dampish ground where it will flourish readily from seed or root cuttings, and thereafter stand for as long as the elves let it. One of its other names is elfdock, through its powers to cure illnesses given to you by naughty elves. The other good news is that its golden blooms are a beacon to fairies, so if you want fairies at the bottom of your garden, elecampane may well offer sufficient attraction.

Fennel, *Foeniculum vulgare*

This perennial, imperishable, rapaciously self-seeding herb has that flavour, somewhere between aniseed and dill, that attracts or repels with no in between. Anyone growing fennel should take the precaution of not allowing it to seed, or you could gather all the seeds (actually fruits) for use before they have the chance to cause mischief. That is unless you are taken with the idea, mentioned by Eleanour Sinclair Rohde, of the disappearing hedge. Should you want, as an acquaintace of Miss S R's did, a shade-giver for the summer only, a fennel hedge can grow to six feet very rapidly, will die back in winter, and will reappear next year even more plentifully.

Fennel's culinary uses need no description here and, given its powers to nullify witches' spells and suchlike, it surely will have a place in most gardens even if the gardener doesn't like aniseed.

William Coles, 1626–1662, was a great student of herbal medicine. In 1657 he published a book usually referred to as *Nature's Paradise* but, in the style of the day, actually titled *Adam in Eden, or, Nature's Paradise: The History of Plants, Fruits, Herbs and Flowers: Withe Their Several Names, Whether Greek, Latin or English, the Places Where They Grow, Their Descriptions and Kinds, Their Times of Flourishing and Decreasing, as also Their Several Signatures,* * *Anatomical Appropriations, and Particular Physical Vertues*. Fennel, Coles says, is 'much used in drinks and broths for those that are grown fat, to abate their unwieldiness and cause them to grow more gaunt and lank'.

Similarly, chewing it is said to assuage hunger, a practice historically of use on fast days but, in modern times, perhaps diet gurus should take note. Be warned, however. Fennel is also classed as a carminative, that is, a substance able to expel wind from the bowels, as in 'Cor, who was that? Who's carminated?' Perhaps the Fennel and Dandelion Diet (see Dandelion, page 116) is what we need to abate our unwieldiness, having taken care to read the instructions.

*Signatures: Coles was an expert in the ancient Doctrine of Signatures, whereby the appearance of plants often designated their use as medicine. So, for example, as a shelled walnut looks like a brain, so God has left us this sign that walnuts are good for that organ.

Fumitory, *Fumaria officinalis*

This is an annual, but such an assertive little seeder that you never will need to help it propagate and can treat it as a perennial. Its pretty, pinky purple, sometimes white flowers are enough to refute its normal status of weed, especially as they last so long, and that's about it, really, unless you want to get rid of freckles, in which case gather up your fumitory ...

> *Whose red and purpled mottled flowers*
> *Are cropped by maids in weeding hours,*
> *To boil in water, milk or whey,*
> *For washes on a holiday;*
> *To make their beauty fair and sleek,*
> *And scare the tan from summer's cheek.*
> John Clare, 1793–1864.

Yellow fumitory, more properly yellow corydalis, is a relative but a native of warmer regions. In and out of gardens, it is often seen clinging to walls, all its small golden trumpets turned to the sun. It has no herbal tradition in Britain.

Germander, *Teucrium spp.*

The germander that herb gardeners tend to grow is *Teucrium chamaedrys*, wall germander, used as an edging plant for its pink flowers and its companiability with a stone edging or low wall. It's a dead-nettle type of plant with aromatic leaves, once used as an air freshener, strewn across the floor, although some would say that the smell is too garlicky for that purpose. Not very hardy, wall germander is not likely to succeed in ungentle climates.

The other germanders are *T. scordium*, water germander, very rare in this country, and *T. scorodonia*, more commonly known as wood sage, growing wild in dry, shady places. Both have a garlicky side to them and, as usual, the family has a long list of ailments against which they are indubitably effective. Wood sage and wall germander are best known for their use in rheumatism and gout.

Horehound, *Marrubium vulgare*

Too bitter to eat and with a strange, musky kind of a smell, white horehound is largely grown for its raggle-taggle looks although it was prized medicinally and was deeply appreciated in East Anglia as the prime ingredient of a kind of beer. In the 1883 parish listing for Holt, in north Norfolk, one Edwin Carter Cooper of the High Street, wine and spirits merchant, also manufactured mineral water and horehound ale.

Early American settlers took it with them from England, to furnish them with medicine against colds and coughs by making a tea of it. Miss Sinclair Rohde quotes Walafrid Strabo as having discovered a use for this herb which is surely unique, and all the more extraordinary when you remember that the squinty old gardener was a monk: 'Drink horehound hot from the fire if you are poisoned by your stepmother.'

This horehound has white flowers and is called white horehound, to distinguish it from black horehound, *Ballota nigra*, which has pink-to-purple flowers. Black horehound stinks when you bruise it. As is often the way with things, the pretty, inoffensive and useful type is now quite rare in Britain, whereas the stinking pinky is common as muck.

Horsetail, mare's tail, hated weed, is used by herbalists in rheumatism and bad circulation, also for chilblains. It contains silicic acid and a horsetail bath is a good way for you to absorb this. Pour very hot water on to a goodly quantity of young horsetail, let it stand for an hour and strain this liquid into your bath. Another good source of silicic acid is red wine.

Horseradish, *Cochlearia armoracia*

Grown since the earliest times for its medicinal uses, horseradish thankfully has now been recognised as the key ingredient of one of the world's greatest sandwiches, viz: liver sausage, beetroot and horseradish. It is also superb with smoked mackerel. The grated root is mixed with fresh cream and a little salt, and there you are. How can you eat roast beef without it? In the late sixteenth century such a thing was unknown in England, according to the distinguished surgeon, author and gardener to Lord Burghley, John Gerard, 1545–1612: 'Horse Radish, stamped with a little vinegar put thereto, is commonly used among Germans for sauce to eate fish with and such like meates as we do mustarde.'

It only took about fifty years from Gerard's notice for horseradish to become popular as a condiment, although only among those not thinking of themselves as 'tender and gentle' in the stomach. The French called it *moutarde des Allemands*, and nowadays Jewish families often eat it at Passover, representative of the bitter-herbs part of the ceremonial meal, to remind them of their sorrows as slaves in Egypt.

Medicinally, not surprisingly, it is seen as a stimulant for the digestion, an antiseptic and a warming reliever of rheumatic and muscular pains.

Houseleek, *Sempervivum tectorum*

Nothing to do with the vegetable, of course, 'leek' coming from the ancient Germanic word for a plant, and looking much more like a dwarf artichoke that's got lost. It is part of the large, succulent family of sedums and stonecrops; once established on a wall or a dry part of the rockery it will stick like glue and spread where you might not believe a plant could survive, by sending out offsets. You can break these off and set the houseleek going somewhere else. It just needs a little earth to give it a start.

The thick, fleshy leaves, or the juice expressed therefrom, are an old and trusted remedy for scalds, spots, bruises and other skin complaints. Next time you are stung by a nettle, try rubbing with a houseleek leaf. That optimistic and versatile proponent of herbal cures, Culpeper, gives it as a corn and wart vanisher and says 'it easeth also the headache, and the distempered heat of the brain in frenzies'.

Hyssop, *Hyssopus officinalis*

This partly evergreen, bushy plant with blue flowers, looking something like a cross between rosemary and a blue dead-nettle, offers sharp, minty young leaves for salads and floral branches to be dried for their aroma or strewn across the floorboards. It's a Mediterranean original so it won't like being put in the cold and damp. The main medicinal uses are for chest complaints.

Pretty enough for a border plant in any flower garden as well as among the herbs, hyssop is beloved of bees and suits a scented garden too. It was used more in cooking in days gone by, when stronger flavours were wanted; no reason why it shouldn't make a comeback.

Lavender, *Lavendula vera*

No question, lavender is the most popular and widely used aromatic herb. This writer's grandmother required nothing more for her Christmas box than a selection of lavender soap and talcum powder, preferably with a spray bottle of lavender water and some lavender bags to put in the linen drawers. A tin of lavender-scented furniture polish would not be given but would be ever-present in the cupboard. A smell of that, of lavender-waxed wood, caught in an old house or an antique shop, guarantees a nostalgic sigh in people of a certain age.

A decoction of lavender flowers, with horehound, fennel, asparagus root and cinnamon is, says Culpeper, 'very profitably used to help turning of the brain'. This writer's own view is that, having gone to the considerable trouble of growing asparagus, one would not dig up the roots for a decoction unless the brain was well and truly turned.

Recent fashion has seen lavender come back as a flavour in restaurant savoury dishes, although said grandmother would have been very surprised at that, if not at the use of its oil during 'her' war, 1914–1918, to clean and heal wounds. Many country folk throughout Europe relied on lavender oil for this purpose and as a staple in all the kinds of physical ailments that result from hard work.

Although not given specifically as a rejuvenator, your aged correspondent notes that it is deemed efficacious against 'Loss of Memory, Dimness of Sight, Melancholy [and] Swooning Fits', and the great man Will Shakespeare hints at the same thing. This is Perdita in *The Winter's Tale*, Act IV, Scene iv:

> *Here's flow'rs for you:*
> *Hot lavender, mints, savory, marjoram;*
> *The marigold, that goes to bed wi' th' sun,*
> *And with him rises weeping; these are flow'rs*
> *Of middle summer, and I think they are given*
> *To men of middle age.*

Edward Lear saw it as a prophylactic as regards the matter of toe loss in Pobbles:

> *His Aunt Jobiska made him drink*
> *Lavender water tinged with pink,*
> *For she said, 'The world in general knows*
> *There's nothing so good for a Pobble's toes!'*

It's as well to grow plenty of it, and perhaps of more than one variety, because people will keep picking it. A fairly poor soil is best, even a stony one over limestone or chalk, but anything will do provided it isn't wet and has plenty of sun. A lavender hedge has to be kept going by a plan of rotation because individual bushes go straggly and leggy after three or four years, so young plants grown from cuttings must be ready each spring to replace them. Take the cuttings in late summer and root them away from frost, preferably in a cold frame or unheated greenhouse.

The last word on this plant, redolent with enchantment of the distant view, must go to Izaak Walton, 1593–1683, he of *The Compleat Angler* and lover of the simple things. His notion of perfection after a day's fishing on the Derbyshire Dove was 'an honest Ale-house where we shall find a cleanly room, Lavender in the Windows'.

Liquorice, *Glycyrrhiza glabra*

This perennial will not stand a hard winter unless the roots are deep in the right kind of soil, which is a light, sandy loam such as you get around Pontefract. A good frost will also kill off the small lengths of root that have been planted to propagate. To be successful, four-feet depth of cultivated, friable soil is required, and the small pieces of root won't give you anything for at least two years. If this is beginning to sound like asparagus in its need for work, that is no coincidence.

The rewards consist of a pretty enough plant, and long roots which can be boiled, and the juice thereof reduced, until it can be made into liquorice bootlaces. Those old enough to remember sweet rationing after the war may also remember buying liquorice root from the chemist's shop, pieces about six inches long for a penny or two, about as thick as a Bic, grey on the outside, bright yellow on the fibrous inside. We chewed away at those roots for hours, for the sweet flavour. It was a simple treat which, like all treats, was a matter relative to the general condition and to the desirability of other known treats, and you just had to put up with the sand.

Lovage, *Levisticum officinale*

This herb has the reverse of the lavender problem; no matter how many people keep picking it, it always seems to grow bigger and bigger. Allegedly reaching 'four feet or even more' (Mrs Grieve), or 'does not attain more than about four feet in height' (Miss Sinclair Rohde), your correspondent states unequivocally that it can attain six feet or more and, if left to itself, will provide you with its own special version of a bamboo jungle. Growing lovage is like having a grove of giant celery-cum-parsley plants, a never-ending source of salad leaves, stalks for cooking, seeds for all sorts, and no possibility of keeping pace with it as it lives for ever and self-seeds profusely.

Lovage has been a food and medicine plant for thousands of years, native to the Mediterranean but quite happy in this country. Indeed, the six-foot giants previously mentioned grew in Westmorland at seven hundred feet above sea level. Medicinally, it is thought to be similar to, but not as good as, angelica, which it looks rather like and is in the same *Umbelliferae* nation. So, it's a stomach settler, a mild laxative, and that's it, really, unless you believe good old Culpeper who says gargling with lovage water cures tonsilitis and drinking same is effectual in pleurisy. Should you have a boil you wish to burst, fry some lovage leaves in a little fat and put them on the boil, still hot. Exactly how hot is up to you. If there is a grumpy, irritating teenage boy of your acquaintance, perhaps you could get him to try this hot-fat-and-lovage cure on his spots.

Lungwort, also called Joseph and Mary and, less romantically, spotted dog, displays flowers of both red and blue. To the old physicians, its leaves looked like lungs and were therefore, according to the Doctrine of Signatures, presumed to be a medicine provided by the gods for lung complaints. This is a cultivated specimen; the same species in the wild is usually more spindly and spare.

Lungwort, *Pulmonaria officinalis*

Soldiers and Sailors, one of lungwort's old names, comes about through the flowers, which show early in the year and start as red like soldiers' coats and turn to a blue-purple as they fully open, and sometimes show both colours at once. More widely known as Jerusalem cowslip, it likes shady nooks and sandy ground.

It's a comfrey/borage/bugloss style of plant but low growing, so good for ground cover, with spotted leaves said to resemble lungs and so designated as a good treatment for lung diseases. Tea made from the dried leaves is given as treatment for coughs, bronchitis and so on, but if it works, that will have more to do with a placebo effect than any virtues in the plant.

Mallows, *Malvaceae spp.*

Some mallows are grown for their flowers but the most important medicinally is the marsh mallow, *Althaea officinalis*, which will manage on ordinary soil but prefers the dampness of its native ditch. It is a softener and a soother, and most of its traditional uses are thus directed, for example in inflammations and irritations. A scratchy cough is relieved in France with the *Tisane des quatre fleurs*, a pleasant-tasting drink made from marsh mallow, borage, violet and poppy.

The common mallow, *Malva sylvestris*, and the musk mallow, *Malva moschata*, have very similar pinky-purple flowers but the musk's are bigger, and it has deeply divided leaves and a musky smell when crushed. The leaves of both can be eaten cooked; both have been used in traditional medicine in places where the rarer marsh mallow will not grow in the wild.

Mandrake, *Atropa mandragora*

Related to the potato and the aubergine, mandrake will not survive a cold British winter and so can only be grown in mild areas. If you can grow it, it will reward you with masses of primula-like flowers and apple-like fruit, but the real mystery is in the root. Like a large parsnip in manured ground, it will tend to fork and, to the fevered imagination, may resemble a long-legged female person.

'Get with child a mandrake root,' said the poet John Donne – alongside exhortations to go and catch a falling star and tell him where all past years are. Should you wish to see if a mandrake plant does have such characteristics, beware, because it will give out a shriek when uprooted, a sound fatal to the person hearing it. The usual way of getting around this was to harness your dog to the job; if it died, it died. If not, it proved that dogs are immune to the mandrake shriek.

That the root was often got up without too many fatalities is shown by the plentiful references to it in the old literature. It was used as a powerful purgative and vomit inducer but also, presumably in a different dose, as a kind of anaesthetic. It could give sleep to a person in discomfort, to such an extent that ancient Greek and Roman surgeons gave bits of root to their patients to chew as a way of easing the pain. Small amounts could expel the demons causing madness, while large amounts could cause madness on their own.

Marjoram, *Oreganum marjorana*

Being more or less hardy, marjoram is a better bet for British gardens than its half-hardy flavour-sibling oregano (pronounced or-EGG-erno, an Italian friend informs us, and not orri-garno). Even so, marjoram will appreciate a little shelter from the worst of winter and in cold districts will not survive without. It does have medicinal uses but we grow it for the kitchen and the salad bowl, where the possibilities are endless.

Said Italian friend also provides us with his recipe for a herby kind of risotto. Follow the basic risotto technique: fry Arborio rice in butter or olive oil, gradually add stock, season, finish with grated Parmesan stirred in with more butter, only add – about two thirds of the way through – a quantity of chopped or torn fresh herbs, a handful per two persons, half marjoram (or oregano) and the rest whatever you have, plus some chopped spring onion and some cashew nuts.

Mints, *Mentha spp.*

Once upon a time, the Greek god Hades, king of the underworld, took a fancy to a nymph called Mentha. In some versions of the story, this happened before he kidnapped his wife and niece Persephone, in some it was after. Anyway, Mentha was far too good looking to be tolerated by wifey, who cast a spell upon her and turned her into a low and creeping plant, to be trodden upon forever. Or it could have been Persephone's mother and Hades' sister, Demeter, who cast the spell, after beating the nymph and kicking her. Hades tried to reverse the spell but could not. So, typical male, he came up with this terrific compromise, of giving the plant a wonderful scent so that, when crushed beneath feet for eternity, she would at least be able to release sweet odours.

Once upon another time, your correspondent decided to have a small mint garden with many different sorts. He had ordinary garden mint of course, and peppermint, apple mint, catmint (living at the time several miles from the nearest cat) and eau-de-Cologne mint. Nearest neighbours were a young couple, she being a decidedly nymphly daughter of an Indian doctor who, as she often described, was a strict type of a fellow, intolerant of faults in others and liable to act in a god-like way.

With doctor father invited to dinner, a blue-moon visit since he lived at a considerable distance and was a very busy god, daughter came round asking for mint, having decided, despite being a cook of modest abilities, to give him trout stuffed therewith. Your correspondent was away at the time, so Madame directed neighbour to the minted region of the garden, not knowing that certain varieties there were unpalatable. The trout cook/nymph, impatient and nervous, was fated to land on the eau-de-Cologne, and so she did. The trout, when presented to father, made him ask why it had been poached in aftershave lotion, and why had his daughter insulted him

Sweet marjoram is a perennial but not an entirely hardy one. It will over-winter only in warmer parts, and in colder with some protection. Marjoram oil is used to relieve the pain of sprains and bruises. Inhaling the steam from a marjoram infusion is said to be good for headaches.

in this way, and if she thought he and her mother were going to stay for another moment she was sadly mistaken.

Eau-de-Cologne mint, *Mentha citrate*, is also called bergamot mint and lemon mint, although the latter name would seem to be something of an understatement. Frances Bardswell writes of 'the most delicious and lasting perfume imaginable; very

In mints, the Big Three are: peppermint, *Mentha x piperata*, a cross between spearmint and watermint, which is variable in looks, often with red, blue or purple tinges; applemint, also called woolly and Egyptian, is actually *M. rotundifolia*, the round-leaved mint; and the one we all know is spear, common or garden mint, *M. spicata*. Rats are alleged to dislike peppermint, so presumably that applies to mice also. Mice cannot resist chocolate, so an exquisite form of mouse torture could be devised by baiting the mousetrap with a piece of Bendicks Bittermint.

distinctive too, less sweet than the scent of Balm, but much more refreshing'. As a young, trout-bearing nymph might have put it, you can say that again.

Spearmint, *M. spicata*, the one we call garden mint, formerly known as lamb mint, is the usual basis for that peculiarly British and Irish version of sweet and sour, mint sauce. Despite its widespread popularity, no food manufacturer seems to have mastered the art and produced a halfway-decent product for sale in shops. That concentrated, macerated silage you can buy in a jar is an abomination. It should never be admitted to your table (you having spent a small fortune on a piece of lamb big enough to roast) and neither should restaurateurs serve it, but they do, the lazy so-and-sos. Your fresh mint is by far superior, and your dried too.

The secret, which is hardly a secret at all, is to make a strong mint tea as the first stage, chopping your fresh or crumbling your dry mint and pouring on just enough boiling water to cover. Allow to stand for a while before adding sugar and vinegar and a pinch of salt. Chopping up the fresh mint with a few grains of sugar or salt will absorb some juice which might otherwise be lost. You could add a small amount of very finely chopped onion, shallot or spring onion, and you could use lemon juice instead of vinegar for a more refined, country-house type of sauce.

So much a part of life was this sauce, when lamb and more especially mutton were cheaper, that a frequent wedding present was a mint chopper, a miniature set of sharp wheel-harrows with a wooden handle instead of a tow-bar, that you rolled across your mint leaves, this way and that. Such a labour-saving device would have come in handy for the harassed mother who, finding her children had dandruff, was advised by grandma that mint sauce was an excellent remedy, made without sugar and massaged into the scalp.

Mint sauce appears to be unknown to the French, so *fromage dur* to them, although they do use mint in the formulation of certain liqueurs such as Benedictine and, obviously, Crème de Menthe, but the association of mint with lamb goes back at least as far as the Exodus of the Jews out of Egypt. The wild mint, *M. arvensis*, also called corn mint, was one of the bitter herbs with which they had to eat the Passover sacrificial lamb, and very memorable that experience must have been. It is likely that the imperial British took spearmint and applemint to India; the Indians, as they would, took it to themselves and sent it back again in a new form. Their combination of yoghurt, mint, sugar, chilli, turmeric and salt can now be found in every Moti Mohal, Star of Bengal or Ul Haq's Kitchen in every town in the UK.

Applemint, so called because to some nasal passages the scent may remind of apples, is *M. rotundifolia*, claimed by some to make the best sauce, although others suggest a mixture of it and spearmint, but all would agree that applemint is the most pleasing of the family to the eye, growing six feet tall in good, moist ground and showing large sprays of pinkish-purple flowers, sometimes also in white. The leaves are covered in tiny white hairs, giving a downy effect in slanted light, and time was when it was known not as apple but as white woolly mint, and before that as Egyptian mint. All mints are refreshing but this one in particular has a stimulating reputation, which would account for its use in one of the more dramatic baths of history.

The Stoic philosopher, playwright, poet, statesman, orator, and tutor to the young Emperor Nero, Lucius Annaeus Seneca, was ordered by the said emperor in later years to end his life, (a) because Nero didn't like anyone to be even slightly more marvellous than himself at anything, and (b) because Seneca was implicated in an assassination plot. Seneca received the news and, unperturbed, decided to do the job by severing veins and arteries but, the story goes, the blood flowed only slowly, giving him much pain rather than the quick, easy death he had imagined. With admirable presence of mind, he ordered a hot bath with Egyptian mint in the water, which would stimulate bloodflow and so permit him to carry out his emperor's wishes more speedily. Once in the bath, he told his friends not to mourn but to live by the ideals of Stoicism, and his wife to find consolation by remembering how lucky she was to have shared his noble life. And so, with words to that effect, Seneca passed away *in pace menthae*.

Peppermint, *M. piperita*, without which we should not have had a mint with a hole, a cigarette as cool as a mountain stream, nor a white, white smile that gets you noticed, is the most cultivated mint commercially. Oil of peppermint has thousands of uses and once was an important manufacture in Britain. The French sometimes call peppermint *menthe Anglaise*, and the most highly regarded variety, black Mitcham, is named for the Surrey town that made it famous. Now, the USA is the main oil maker, with just a few specialists in the UK.

All the mints are sources of menthol but the main one for menthol crystals is *M. arvensis*, corn mint, much cultivated in India for making those crystals by natural methods, although absolutely loathed by peppermint farmers because it gets in the crop and ruins the oil. The demand for menthol crystals far exceeds India's output and much of it is made synthetically. Menthol does not always suit very young children, so preparations of peppermint and corn mint should not be given.

Corn mint was the one most accused of interfering with cheesemaking, which might explain why India is not famous for cheese, although all mints were supposed to prevent milk curdling; milk from cows that had been eating wild hedgerow mints would not separate into curds and whey and so would not make cheese. Such a headache for the dairymaids might be cured by inhaling the aroma of peppermint, although this did little to remedy the no-cheese situation.

Mint tea is a well-known tummy settler; peppermint and spearmint are ingredients in commercial digestifs and heartburn remedies. Menthol in ointments, sometimes combined with eucalyptus and pine extracts, is widely applied externally for aches and stiffness, and inhaled it relieves chest complaints.

To the four herbs of Scarborough Fair – parsley, sage, rosemary and thyme – add mint and you have the five herbs no kitchen garden can do without. Pennyroyal is a mint but is dealt with on its own, below.

Mugwort, *Artemisia vulgaris*

Why would you want to grow a herb with such an uncivilised name, which grows abundantly in the wild and is not especially decorative? Good question. Possibly you might want your own guaranteed supply for use as a tonic, or you may want to give it to your footman as William Coles recommended in his *Art of Simpling*, so that the servant could put it in his shoes and walk forty miles before noon and never feel a thing. Obviously it would be even better in Paula Radcliffe's trainers as she only does 26 miles 385 yards. It would have been even better than that for poor old Pheidippides in 490 BC, the Olympic champion who ran, swam rivers and climbed mountains for four days, from Athens to Sparta and back, to enlist the Spartans in aid against the Persians. After the battle, he carried the news of victory from Marathon to Athens, only to drop dead as he did so. Marathon to Athens is actually about twenty-two miles, so entrants to the

London and other famous city marathons who don't quite get there can always say that at least they did as well as Pheidippides, apart from the four days beforehand.

The leaves and the roots of mugwort are dried and used as an emmenagogue. On behalf of those very few readers who don't know what an emmenagogue is, this writer has already looked it up in the *Oxford English Dictionary* and it means a substance that encourages menstrual flow. It is also a diaphoretic – it encourages perspiration – so, with all that encouragement and some mugwort in your shoes, you need never look back.

The Anglo-Saxons' word is *mucgwyrt*, who also called it *matrum herba*, mother-herb in Latin. They thoroughly believed the footman story and expected it to look after them on wearisome journeys.

Mullein, *Verbascum thapsus*

A biennial but no trouble to propagate, this space-rocket of a plant is well worth a place at the back of the class. From a flat rosette of furry leaves in the first year, it sends up a spike with leaves gradually getting smaller and terminating in a wondrous head of yellow flowers. In the wild it can reach five feet. In your garden, looked after, expect it to make seven or even eight feet. It doesn't like the wet and has adapted itself to growing in dry regions, so treat it accordingly.

Mullein tea, made from the leaves, is a really ancient remedy for chesty complaints, but you must, must sieve it carefully, because those hairs that make the leaves so furry will drive you mad if they get in your mouth. Curiously, smoking the dried leaves, in a pipe or a roll-up, is supposed to stop that irritating cough.

Long, long before the products of Messrs L'Oréal, Max Factor, Boots etc. became available, those ladies of Rome who were dissatisfied with their hair colour (and conscious of the oft-quoted maxim that gentlemen prefer blondes) would wash their hair in a strong infusion made with the flowers of mullein mixed with wood ash. Burning the plant itself, which is a very easy matter, makes ashes which were also used on the hair in an attempt to restore that which was grey to its former glory.

An old and rather interesting idea is to make mullein oil, by steeping the flowers for several weeks in plain olive oil. The result is claimed to be a germ killer and good for cuts, bruises and inflammation. Those whose style of life over a lengthy period has developed in them both the piles and the gout should be cheered by the mullein, as tea from the flowers can alleviate the latter while the above-mentioned oil can deal with the former.

And finally, mullein seeds have for centuries been used to catch fish. Something in the seeds was observed to render fish senseless and easy to take. Those Roman gentlewomen lightening their hair colour may also have been gratified to find themselves free of nits because that 'something' is rotenone, known for many years to gardeners as derris, now banned from sale by the health and safety industry. It is a powerful killer of insects and mites and, therefore, of fish, while being generally harmless when ingested by humans.

Pennyroyal, *Mentha pulegium*

Smells nice, tastes awful – these are qualities that partly account for the reverence in which it has always been held, although its official name comes from its supposed ability to drive fleas away, from the Latin *pulex*, a flea.

The usual variety, *M. p. decumbens*, is a low-growing, sprawling plant, much smaller than the other mints, used in some herb gardens as a green path to give off odours when trodden. It needs to be in a dampish part of the garden because pennyroyal will not stand drought.

Dioscorides and the other ancients commended it for all sorts of ailments, and good old Nick Culpeper also waxed lyrical, prescribing it as a drink to cure whooping cough and leprosy, and as a poultice with salt when 'it profits those that are splenetic'. This is an intriguing thought. You make a poultice with a bit of mint and you go up to your splenetic person who, by nature of his condition, is morose, peevish, testy and ill-humoured, and … what do you say?

Pennyroyal's chief and more realistic virtues concern menstrual distress and disturbance. Traditionally in Britain it has been grown to make a tea, an old remedy for period pains and related disorders. Regular doses of a strong version of this tea would be given to terminate a pregnancy; if overdone there could be damage to liver and kidneys, possibly fatal. Even so, another long-standing use has been for digestive upsets in children, as a gripe water.

Periwinkle, *Vinca major*

Most people grow this in the herb garden as ground cover, it being a most tenacious and intolerant plant, its very name meaning to encircle and bind. It flowers very early in the year, is a pretty blue with shiny leaves, and deserves its place for that alone. It doesn't generally seed in this country but has no need, since its spreading stems will root at the slightest opportunity.

Well, that's what most people do with periwinkle. It is also used as a laxative, and gargling with periwinkle tea can be good for sore throats, but that's fairly mundane stuff when you consider what some of our ancestors got up to. They dried it and ground it up with earthworms and houseleek, and put it in their beloved's dinner in cases where the beloved had grown cool of late. We cannot doubt the efficacy of this procedure for a moment, but we must ask if periwinkle, gathered when the moon is nine nights old (or eleven, thirteen or one), will be proof as claimed against poisoning and demoniacal possession.

Sir Thomas More came to a sorry end at the orders of Henry VIII but, in happier times, he wrote a few simple words about rosemary: 'I let it run all over my garden walls, not only because my bees love it, but because it is the herb sacred to remembrance, and, therefore, to friendship.'

Rosemary, *Rosmarinus officinalis*

For weakness and coldness of the brain, a good remedy is to boil rosemary in wine and inhale the vapours. Or, you could put it on the barbecue with the garlicky lamb chops and inhale it that way, which will surely strengthen any brain, at least in a determination to get at those chops.

As with all the major herbs, there are legends and superstitions unnumbered, from the banishment of bad dreams by rosemary under the bed, to the extent of its growth in a garden being an indicator of who wore the trousers in the house.

As the young gentlemen of Edison Lighthouse sang in 1970, 'Love grows where my Rosemary goes,' and a good way to entrance your lover might be to serve him or her with an old-fashioned rosemary sauce, rarely seen nowadays but very good with lamb.

Chop a small onion finely and sweat it in butter. Add some flour, a well-heaped tablespoon, and stir away any lumps as you introduce half a pint or so of stock. Bring to the boil and add a few rosemary leaves. Simmer for ten minutes and taste. Add more leaves if you want, plus salt and pepper, simmer for another few minutes, take the pan off the heat, and leave for a few minutes more. Beat an egg yolk and add a small amount of the sauce thereto. Add some more, and keep adding, and stirring, until you have used about half your onion and rosemary sauce. Throw your egg mix back into the pan with the rest of the sauce, warm gently, do not boil, and serve.

Rue, *Ruta graveolens*

Although eaten and commended by everyone in the Olden Days, rue provokes disagreement in modern times. Some say the smell is foul and the flavour fouler, and there is no doubting that any child would much prefer Brussels sprouts. Others view it as strong, yes, aggressive even, but an acquired taste. It is just about the bitterest thing you can grow; it may not outrank wormwood in pure bitterness but its extra power has it at least reaching first equal. The floral-minded love its special blue-green leaves that stay aglimmer in the dark days of winter and this is probably the main reason you might want to grow it.

It certainly exemplifies the belief, universally held in times when pills went unsugared, that the worse tasting the medicine, the more likely it was to do you good. All the ancient writers praised it to the skies and assigned a great many qualities to it, including some magical ones. It was used in exorcisms and in other ways to prevent or expel evil spirits, but its established uses have mainly been in chest and stomach complaints and as a general stimulant. In the unlikely event of your eating too much of it, you may throw up. Rue tea should therefore be avoided after meals.

Our word rue, in the sense of penitence, sorrow and regret, has nothing to do with our word rue, meaning the herb. The former is the same as the Anglo-Saxon *hreow*; the latter is from Latin *ruta*, meaning the plant and, for the poets, bitterness. Also nothing to do with rue is goat's rue, *Galega officinalis*, which is related to peas and beans.

A big and vigorous plant with long spikes of flowers, rue will do well with the other stately herbs. It must be included in the medicinal list because it is given as a galactagogue, which, contrary to all our expectations, is not a means of reaching for the furthermost stars, as might be the case with some other herbal substances. Our prop and stay, the *OED*, tells us a galactagogue is an encouragement to milk flow in nursing mothers. There you are: *Classic Herb Garden*, increasing the nation's infant-feeding capacity and vocabulary at the same time.

Sage, *Salvia officinalis*

The bees of Croatia make some of the best honey in the world from it. Italian chefs put it in their saltimbocca. The French pile it on pork fillet with loads of garlic and butter. The Turks make a liver pilaff with it. The British buy boxes of breadcrumb sawdust with specks of it mixed in, pour water on said sawdust and stuff it up a cardboard chicken. To be fair, we also put it in Canard à la Pavilly and Derbyshire cheese.

Sage needs a little more attention in the garden than the other perennials, although it's hardy enough for most UK regions despite being a native of the Mediterranean. It does tend to go straggly and semi-dead after two or three years, so constant renewal by cuttings or layering is necessary to keep up a supply of this essential. Light soil and a warm place with partial shade is the ideal.

About 500 members of the salvia family were known by the 1930s but the number is now nearer 700. They are native to the New World and the Old, in the more temperate areas, offering flowers and leaves of many colours. For our purposes, unless looking for half-hardy glory as with *S. splendens*, a Brazilian in scarlet, we can concentrate on four: the standard culinary *S. officinalis*; clary sage, *S. scalrea*; and, for the perfumed garden, *S. greggii* and *S.microphylla/grahamii*, both Mexicans. *Greggii* is also called autumn sage although it blooms in summer too. Both species have many cultivars and may cross-breed, in which case you could have your own private salvia.

Sage tea can be made with the leaves and/or the flowers, two handfuls to the pint of water, giving you a beverage that was widely thought to be at least as refreshing as proper tea, especially if a little sugar and lemon were added. If we go back to times before we knew about cups of China and Indian, those country folk apparently believed that sage tea twice a day, or sage eaten with bread, would make them live longer. As a gargle it is meant to cure sores and other afflictions of the mouth and throat, in which case you can use half and half vinegar and water rather than neat water.

As usual with a herb that has an easily observable action – and everyone will agree on the cheering virtues of sage tea if not on the life-prolonging ones – a great many further and less credible abilities are ascribed to sage. Dioscorides says it gives ease in urinating to those who find that difficult, and it can turn your hair black. He's not alone on the hair-dying front; that's a tradition followed for centuries after the old boy died, having failed to cure himself of more serious ills that may have included plague, consumption, memory loss and the stitch, all of which Culpeper states can be relieved by use of sage.

The culinary association is always sage with pork, poultry and veal, as mint with lamb, and most felicitous are the dishes resulting. Here is a recipe for pork and sage balls, adapted from the medieval original to make it possible in the modern kitchen. To a pound (500 grams or so) of finely minced raw pork add a small handful of breadcrumbs or coarse oatmeal, and two eggs. Season with salt and pepper and

Salad burnet was once an important medicinal herb, being good against a trembling or shaking heart, but now is grown only as a leafy ingredient of interesting salads and drinks.

powdered ginger, add a handful of chopped sage leaves and knead all together. Form into rissoles and fry gently on both sides.

Salad burnet, *Poterium sanguisorba*

Poterium means goblet, *sorbeo* means I sup up or suck in, and *sanguis* is blood, so this innocent little wild plant was named for a reputation quite different from its modern one. In fact, the ancients thought very highly of it as a wound-healer and it still is said to be a styptic, but those pretty little leaves, slightly cucumber-ish in taste, are best grown for culinary use. Add them to dishes where you might add chives. Put them in a salad or sprinkle them on summer drinks such as Pimm's.

Salad burnet will self-seed, but remove flowers and older leaves to encourage fresh growth and see it grow into a pretty mound. It is much hardier than it looks and will offer you green leaves right through winter, although they may well be rather bitter by then. The plant doesn't like it too wet or too acidic; average soil is fine, or worse than that is better.

Santolina, *Santolina chamaecyparissus*

Usually called lavender cotton, or cotton lavender, it is neither cotton nor lavender but a small, evergreen shrub of the huge tribe *Compositae* which includes the daisies, the thistles, the dandelion types, the marigolds and the chamomiles, not to mention the creeping cudweed of Ben Vorlich. Santolina has yellow flowers like tansy and silvery grey foliage, which makes it useful as an edging plant. As with avens, you can circumvent the mothball police by using dried santolina.

Sorrel, *Rumex acetosa*

There's no great mystery to growing sorrel. It's happy pretty well anywhere, although will naturally thrive better in a rich, well-drained soil with a fair amount of sun. It is an outstanding addition to green salads and will lend flavour to those boring tomatoes you have to buy in the spring before yours are ready. There is a milder version, *R. scutatus*, also called French or wimps' sorrel, so grow that if you must.

Medicinally, sorrel is seen as a livener and thirst quencher. Culpeper of course is mad about it, saying it will cool any inflammation, refresh the overspent spirits, procure an appetite in fainting or decaying stomachs and resist the poison of the scorpion. It certainly refreshes the spirits early in the year when there is so little else green and edible to cheer about in the garden.

Sorrel leaves chopped as fine as possible, with a little wine vinegar and sugar, make a perfect sauce to serve with roast pork when you have no apples in the larder. Cooked with butter and cream or yoghurt it goes well with plain oily fish, also smoked eel, smoked mackerel and the like. You can make a pesto with it, or use it instead of parsley in a wine or béchamel sauce to liven up a piece of dull fish such as pollack or coley.

Sorrel cheese

Into a pint of whole milk put a good dollop of single cream, a pinch or two of salt, the juice of half a lemon and a handful of chopped sorrel leaves. Bring slowly up to blood heat or so, stirring gently, and take off the heat when the curds and whey separate. Sieve through muslin or similar, reserving the whey for another purpose such as liquid for a curry, and hang the muslin cheesebag where it can drip for an hour or two.

The lemon is insurance against there not being enough acid in the sorrel to curdle the milk. You could experiment with more sorrel and with sorrel juice. When the cheese has finished dripping, add some fresh, finely chopped sorrel and perhaps a little chopped spring onion.

If you were to make a decent quantity and really squeeze it dry, you could make a version of *mattar paneer*, which is peas stir-fried in butter with turmeric, cayenne and salt for a few minutes, with the special sorrel cheese added at the last.

Southernwood, *Artemesia abrotatum*

Another for the scented garden, southernwood is the wormwood from the south, that is, not native to this country. It flowers rarely here and it is for the unique scent of the leaves that it is grown now, although it was highly regarded for other properties. Bees and other insects don't seem to like it even when it does have flowers, so it was used to keep moths away, but it is also credited as a boon to spotty youth and that is what gives it the common name of lad's love.

Readers will be thrilled to know that this herb, southernwood, is valued as an anthelmintic and a deobstruent, which is to say it kills intestinal worms while it opens the natural passages of the body. The latter feature goes with the former and lets the dead worms out.

Boil the leaves with barley meal, said the old wife, and you will have a mudpack for the erupting adolescent who wishes to appear less repulsive in the eyes of she-who-is-adored. He may also include some fresh southernwood sprigs in the bouquet of flowers he gives her, for the scent, but there is a danger here. If she has listened to her mother, she will know that the chief medicinal use of southernwood is as an emmenagogue, which is the one that brings on the monthly period.

Ah well, young love is a wonderful thing, but should the acnefied sub-adult also wish to seem older, he can burn some southernwood, mix the ashes with lard or oil, and rub his chinny-chin-chin with it in the hope of promoting designer stubble. Later in life, when the trials of living with she-who-was-adored have made his hair fall out, restoration can be attempted with the same treatment. Meanwhile she, at church and listening to a sermon from the most boring man on this earth, can keep herself awake by sniffing at her posy of southernwood.

Miss Sinclair Rohde recommends growing southernwood as a neat bush, ruthlessly pruned every spring by cutting each branch back to two buds. Should you want more, or to rear some plants for gifts or sale, the prunings will make good cuttings if mostly stripped and planted deep in a sandy compost.

Sweet cicely, *Myrrhis odorata*

Looking at first sight like another one of all those parsleys, chervils, caraways and wild parsnips, sweet cicely does deserve a place in the herb garden for its scent, vaguely reminiscent of incense with a hint of anise; for its seeds, which used to be a source of furniture polish; and for its handsome looks when fully grown to four or five feet. It lives

Sweet cicely has its name from the Latin *seselis*, by which the Romans indicated Mediterranean hartwort, which does look a bit like sweet cicely. *Seselis* could also mean meadow saxifrage, which looks nothing like sweet cicely. The girl's name came afterwards.

a long time and grows slowly, but meantime offers young leaves for salads and the seeds too, when green, are a spicy addition.

The seeds, or fruits, are oily and perfumed, so when mature can be crushed and rubbed into your farmhouse pine. You are unlikely to dig up this fine plant for its root but, if you did, you could make an infusion of it which, Mrs Grieve mysteriously informs us, makes a valuable tonic for girls of fifteen to eighteen years of age. Bearing in mind the progress of the human race since 1930, we should probably recalculate that as girls of eleven to fourteen.

Tansy, *Tanacetum vulgare*

The dessert now commonly called a tansy, lying somewhere between an omelette and a custard, is a combination of eggs and cream with fruit that never has any tansy in it. Earlier tansies, traditionally eaten at Easter for reasons variously given, had their sharpness in the sweet from tansy juice and, sometimes, spinach juice, and could be in a pastry case like a quiche. The original tansy cakes were probably just scrambled eggs and tansy leaves.

Tansy requires no special treatment in the garden, being happy to grow anywhere, so happy in fact that some authorities think it more suited to the village common. Medicinally, its main use was in 'expelling worms from children', as Mrs Grieve puts it. In days before refrigerators, those who could afford meat in quantity, so that it needed to be kept for a time after delivery from the butcher, would have a member of the kitchen staff rub tansy on it so as to deter flies.

Not everyone will want to give this large and vigorous plant, tansy, space in a garden, but if your refrigerator should break down you may want some to rub on your meat.

Tarragon, *Artemisia dracunculus*

A perennial in warmer climes, tarragon needs some protection against our winters and will tend to fizzle out after a very few years anyway, so young plants should be reared from cuttings or root divisions to maintain a supply. A root in a pot in the greenhouse will supply some leaves for the dark days.

Tarragon vinegar is the famous thing, the only true vinegar with which to make tartare sauce. It's nothing more than tarragon leaves steeped in best wine vinegar for a fortnight then strained off. Usually more, fresh, stems are put in the bottle to identify it and make it look nice.

The slightly coconutty flavour of the herb has a particular affinity for chicken. You might like to try frying chicken pieces in French butter which, as every downstairs cook used to know, is butter, lemon juice, tarragon vinegar and fresh tarragon (or parsley and tarragon mixed), creamed together. Allow half a lemon, a teaspoon of vinegar and a tablespoon of fresh herb to each quarter pound (125 grams, about) of salted butter.

Tarragon does not have a strong medicinal tradition but doesn't need one when you have the other artemisias – mugwort, southernwood and wormwood.

Tarragon chicken soufflé

Not a recipe for the fainthearted, although most of it can be done well beforehand, so that guests will be amazed at the production of something so classy in twenty minutes with little intervention from the cook. This is lunch for four, served with a potato salad and a green or tomato salad.

First stage: roast a medium-sized chicken, strip off the meat so you have a thin pound or around 400 grams, roughly chopped. Make a strong chicken stock with the carcase and a sprig or two of tarragon.

Make a white sauce with half milk, half chicken stock. You want about half a pint of finished sauce.

Put the chicken in the bottom of a deep, ovenproof dish, season, pour over the sauce. Turn the meat so it's mixed in.

In a double boiler/bain Marie, add a teaspoon of arrowroot to three tablespoons of chicken stock and bring up to thickening temperature. Off the stove, stir in a quarter of a bar of butter (what we used to call two ounces), three tablespoons of double cream, a tablespoon of chopped tarragon, a splash of Worcester, salt and pepper.

Separate the yolks from the whites of three eggs, and beat the yolks. Stir them into the warm butter/cream mix and gently heat, still in the bain Marie. Keep stirring until it thickens. Allow to cool to room temperature but don't refrigerate. That's the prep done.

With 25 minutes to go, turn your oven on to 175°C/Regulo 4, and while it's heating, beat your egg whites to stiff peaks. Fold the whites into the mix, pour over the sauced chicken, and put in the oven for fifteen minutes or a little longer.

Sauce estragonaise

This is an old-fashioned English version of what we imagined the French might serve with white fish, and it works jolly well if a little fiddly to prepare. It's basically a béarnaise/hollandaise with tarragon added. Put an ounce of plain flour, two of butter, an egg yolk and a good dollop of French mustard in a double boiler and, over a gentle heat, slowly add a half pint of single cream. When that's melted, add a small handful of chopped tarragon and a very finely chopped spring onion. Season and stir over the steam. When you have a sauce as you like it, stir a little longer to make it slightly thicker, then add a spot or two of lemon juice.

A cruder if quicker and more fail-safe method would be to make a béchamel with cream instead of milk and add the tarragon, lemon and onion to that.

Thyme, *Thymus spp.*

There are several wild thymes in the UK and many cultivated ones, all of which offer an aromatic ingredient in the kitchen, a pretty, spreading plant for the herb garden and an irresistible temptation for bees. Thyme likes things dry and sunny, which makes it ideal for rocky parts, walls and crazy-paved paths, where different types with variously coloured leaves and flowers can tumble and spread and fill the air with sweet scents. Older plants need to be divided or replaced as they lose their matting quality and/or start to straggle.

Those ubiquitous presences in herbal lore, 'country folk', were wont to put the dried flowers of thyme and rosemary in with their winter clothes when storing for the summer, and lavender too. This was, allegedly, to repel insects. One must suspect that the country folk were actually seeking the perfume, for they would surely know better than to imagine that flowers so attractive to insects when fresh would become repellent to them when dried, and it must be the modern commentators who assign this custom at their desks without really thinking about it.

The most planted species are ordinary garden thyme, *T. vulgaris*, and lemon thyme, *T. citriodorus*, which has several varieties including the golden-leaved type, but there are enough thymes from different countries and climates, with sufficient alternative requirements, to make a complete garden specialisation.

Thyme on culinary duty goes with anything tomatoey. It's marvellous in salad dressings and is a key ingredient in a Madeira sauce that used to be served with veal or kidneys, or indeed veal kidneys, at country house weekends. To some chicken stock add

Oil of thyme, through its constituent thymol, has antiseptic and antifungal properties and was used in this way long before such matters were properly understood. It could be seen to work; knowing why and how didn't matter, or could be claimed as a proof of magical powers. Mrs Grieve says that an infusion of thyme is 'useful in cases of drunkenness' but does not give details as to how it should be administered nor what might be expected by way of beneficial results.

chopped onion, carrot and tomato. Cook until all is well done, and sieve. Make a roux. Pour in your sieved base plus fresh parsley and thyme, stir to a thickness and add a goodly slosh of Madeira. You could, if you wished, add some crumbled crispy bacon and a touch of chilli, and use sherry instead of Madeira, whereupon the sauce changes countries and becomes Spanish.

Spaghetti alla Helena

Before the days of Italian cookery books and pizza palaces, the good old British were aware of spaghetti, or at least the upper classes were, having been to Italy on the grand tour, but they didn't quite know what to do with it. So, as we did with Indian food, deciding that anything was a curry if you put Vencatachellum's curry powder in it (the pink or the blue tin, didn't matter), so the cooks in the big houses decided that sauce Hélène was the thing for pasta and a light lunch. Fry onion, garlic and tomatoes in butter, having skinned the toms of course, and add minced veal or chicken. Cook for as long as you like, adding white wine as you go and reducing. You could put in some tomato puree too. At the death, add thyme leaves and cream cheese, stir, and serve.

Valerian, *Valeriana officinalis*

Famous as a soporific and sedative, the root of valerian, generally harvested in its second year, is widely cultivated and processed today, mostly in Europe and largely in Germany where it is very popular as a remedy for insomnia. It grows wild pretty well everywhere but demand exceeds the supply of people who are willing to go out and get it. It used to be a speciality of Derbyshire, where the 'valerie growers' could make a bit of extra cash on top of their miners' wages. Possibly because it makes you drowsy, valerian was assigned a number of roles in the treatment of nervous disorders including Parkinson's disease, then known as St Vitus's Dance, but that does not explain why the Scots of old put it in their porridge.

Vervain, *Verbena officinalis*

Closely related to but not much like all those verbenas people put in hanging baskets, wild vervain is a fairly undistinguished plant in looks but of great interest otherwise. After the crucifixion of Jesus, spices, ointments, myrrh and aloes are mentioned in the Bible as treatment of the body, but the tradition is that vervain was used to staunch the wounds. Thus it has the name 'herb of grace' which, added to the repute it already had among the ancients, was enough to propel it into the 'heals everything' category.

The priests of the Greek, Roman and British pre-Christian and non-Abrahamic religions used it in their ceremonies and sacrifices. Medieval witches and wise-women were likely to mix it in love potions, and their modern equivalents still do. A teaspoon of vervain, with the same of lovage and basil, brewed with nutmeg and red wine and accompanied by magic words, will make the desired one fall for the brewer. Magic words are incorporated into an easily memorised framework of doggerel and usually include moon, boon, bright and tonight. Modern herbalists, however, recommend it as a preventative of kidney stones but not much else.

Winter savory, *Satureia montana*

Hardier and more shrub-like than its summer namesake, winter savory is a strongly flavoured sweet herb that prefers the poorer, drier sort of ground to rich bedding. In the right place it will reward you with a fine show of white flowers and will be evergreen, but will not last many seasons and so cuttings or layerings should be taken regularly to keep up supplies.

It has no real medicinal tradition except as a comfort for insect stings. Miss Sinclair Rohde says that 'country folk know the value of Savory for rubbing on wasp and bee stings', although its benefits against both acidic and alkaline irritants would have to be determined by experience.

Woad, *Isatis tinctoria*

It is hard to find a good reason for growing this self-seeding biennial. In flower, to the man on the galloping horse it looks like rape or any other member of the cabbage family, and it cannot be used for much outside of its famous abilities in dying. Before the introduction of indigo, woad was a very important blue dye and there was a woad industry all over Europe and elsewhere, but that gradually fell away and had disappeared almost entirely by the end of the First World War.

The last British woad mill closed in the 1930s but renewed interest from those with flower-power tendencies has seen a small revival and a new woad farm and processing facility in Norfolk. This is not very far from one of the old centres of the industry in Wisbech, where they used to sing this woad-gathering song, implying perhaps the wealth to be acquired if you were to keep right on to the end of the woad:

Molly of the Woad and I fell out,
O, what do you think it was all about?
For she had money and I had none,
And that is how the strife begun.

Another member of the cabbage tribe, woad has the usual yellow flowers but, uniquely, blue-purple seed pods. The blue dye Julius Caesar witnessed as British war paint is made from the young green leaves, which are twice fermented in a precise and complicated process smelling very strongly of, well, rotting cabbage leaves. Although the song tells us that 'Woad's the stuff to show men, Woad to fright the foemen,' that may have been its secondary purpose, the main one possibly a kind of healing in advance: a precaution against infection and loss of blood when wounded.

Woodruff, *Galium odoratum*

This rather dainty perennial has a gardening use as one to fill shady places and as an attraction for bees. It actively dislikes lots of sunshine, being a native of damp woodland, but its neatly arranged circles of leaves and small white flowers can cover awkward spots under trees, especially beech and ash. However, it does produce seed balls with hooks, so your questing Jack Russell or cat may well come in with lots attached.

It has little scent when growing but that increases with drying, and this led to one of its main benefits as a herb – to be hung in bunches to sweeten the air.

Sweet woodruff, a plant that goes pale in open sunlight, contains a substance called coumarin, a toxic benzopyrone which is the precursor for warfarin. Curiously, the herb used to be recommended for healing wounds and for liver diseases, while warfarin is nowadays prescribed as an anticoagulant and is moderately poisonous, especially to liver and kidneys.

Wormwoods, *Artemisia spp.*

Queen Henrietta Maria, wife of Charles I, mother of Charles II and James II, had a cook known now only as 'W M' whose method for wormwood wine was to steep two pounds of the whole plant in two gallons of Rhenish for a quarter of a year or more, then strain and bottle. The modern equivalent would be a handful of wormwood leaves in a bottle of hock. Wormwood brandy, made by infusing an ounce of flowers in a pint of the spirit for six weeks, was recommended by Dr John Hill in 1772 as a reliever of gout, apparently from personal experience.

Dr Hill, a famous actor, playwright, botanist and London character, also said it would prevent the increase of gravel, which sounds odd until you realise that the gravel in question is the crystals formed in the urine by gout-inclined persons, usually men who drink too much port and brandy, which may then develop into bladder stones.

Which of the wormwoods to use with wine and brandy is not specified. Common wormwood, *Artemisia absinthium*, is acknowledged the strongest in flavour, sea wormwood the next, *A. maritima*, also called Old Woman, followed by Roman wormwood, *A. pontica*, which is the most likely for wine.

All are tonics. Those country folk, should they live to a remarkably old age, would sometimes ascribe this to regular intake of Roman wormwood flower tea and, while wormwood is a biblical and literary byword for bitterness, it is said to stimulate the appetite and deal with disorders of the stomach.

Chapter Three

Herbs from Seeds

Anise, *Pimpinella anisum*

This is a tender annual, unlikely to ripen its seeds unless it is planted in a favourable spot in full sun, and we have a really good summer. As it is the seeds that are of use, as a spice and flavouring, also in coughs, chest ailments and flatulence, you might be better off with dill and fennel.

On the other hand, should a wedding impend, you may wish to recreate the only truly traditional wedding cake. The Romans, at the end of a feast, ate a cake as a digestif called *mustaceum*, which was made with young wine and herbs including anise and cumin, and baked on bay leaves. Some of the biggest feasts were at weddings and so the word *mustaceum* came to mean wedding cake. Possibly, guests at a wedding today would be surprised to be given a piece of cake tasting of aniseed, but the Roman proverb arising from it might be highly appropriate if the *Hello!* magazine photographer were there: *Laureolam in mustaceo quaerere*, to look for a laurel wreath in cake, that is, to seek for fame out of trifles.

Basil, *Ocimum spp.*

The two main species are bush basil, *O. minimum*, the low-growing, small-leaved type, and sweet basil, *O. basilicum*, larger all round. Neither will stand our winters and so must be grown as half-hardy annuals, in which case sweet basil is the obvious one to go for. The flavours are very similar, although fussy Italians apparently prefer bush basil for pesto.

Sweet basil is often grown as a pot plant, as it frequently used to be – the aroma being credited with procuring a cheerful and merry heart. Thomas Tusser emphasises its tenderness:

Fine basil desireth it may be her lot,
To grow as the gilliflower, trim in a pot;
That ladies and gentles to whom ye do serve
May help her, as needeth, poor life to preserve.

Another rather better poet, John Keats, also took inspiration from a basil plant, trim in a pot. His fourteenth-century beauty Isabella took a lover of whom her brothers

African blue basil is a hybrid variety of sweet basil and so must be grown from cuttings. Like all basils it is really a perennial but needs to be protected if it's to last out our winters. This is one mainly for the floral benefits; it's not the best for flavouring but cut flowers last well.

disapproved. They killed the lad in the woods. Isabella worked out where, searched, found the body and cut off the head. She took it home and put it in the bottom of a large pot, covered it with the medieval equivalent of John Innes, and planted some basil.

And so she ever fed it with thin tears,
Whence thick, and green, and beautiful it grew.

In more recent times, basil fell out of favour for a while, perhaps because of the slight bother with growing it, but the upsurge of interest in food has made it an essential. Fresh basil in a tomato salad cannot be equalled and might have been the only end in view a few years ago. Now you can get Thai basil, lemon basil, special spicy basils, different colours – one seed merchant in the UK offers over thirty varieties at the time of writing.

There is little medical tradition with basil although it is venerated by Hindus as a protection against the ills of the world. The ancient European beliefs were more to do with scorpions, and otherwise perfectly sensible people believed that these arachnids could spring forth from basil mistreated.

Caraway, *Carum carvi*

The seeds are the target here, so plants have to be nurtured into their second season from spring sowings. Autumn sowings will produce a crop at the end of the following summer. It has similar digestif properties to the other aniseedy herbs of the great *Umbelliferae* tribe but is grown for its culinary uses, which historically has meant seed cake.

Not everyone likes seed cake, and they probably wouldn't like the roots either, which look like little parsnips but taste, unsurprisingly, of caraway. The best use of caraway in your correspondent's view is in the excellent liqueur made by the Dutch, the Germans and the Russians, called Kümmel. You can make your own version of this with vodka, caraway seed, fennel seed, ground cumin and sugar, and very interesting it might turn out to be, but if you're going to buy good vodka for it, you might as well buy the real thing.

Those old country folk used to grind the seeds with new breadcrumb, held together with something spiritous, and stuff the result into any aching ear, which was supposed to effect a wondrous cure, and it may have done.

King Henry IV Part Two, Act V, Scene iii. Enter Falstaff, Shallow, Silence, Bardolph, the Page, and Davy.

Justice Shallow: *Nay, you shall see my orchard where, in an arbour, we shall eat a last year's pippin of mine own graffing, with a dish of caraways, and so forth.*

PUNCH'S FANCY PORTRAITS.—No. 97.

SIR JOHN LUBBOCK, M.P., F.R.S.

How doth the Banking Busy Bee
Improve his shining Hours
By studying on Bank Holidays
Strange Insects and Wild Flowers!

According to Miss Bardswell, Sir John Lubbock, first president of the Institute of Bankers and a noted botanist, observed the insects visiting his caraway flowers, which are too small for many would-be honey tasters. He counted fifty-five visitors: one moth, nine bees, twenty-one flies and twenty-four midges.

The 'so forth' doubtless referred to great quantities of wine. The pippin would have been roasted; you took a bite and dipped the exposed apple-flesh in a saucer of caraway seeds, ready for the next person.

Cacen Gneifo

This is the Welsh shearing cake, eaten at sheep shearing, with as many variations in the recipe as there are Welsh farmers' wives. (Note on sexual equality: even in these liberated days, you are very unlikely to find a sheep farmer, Welsh, Dales, Cumbrian, Scottish or otherwise, baking cakes unless, of course, the farmer is female. Anyone wishing to protest this view of agricultural reality should send a slice of Cacen Gneifo to the author, c/o the publisher.)

All bakers agree on one ingredient and that's caraway seeds. Thus we have, for example: 8oz/225g plain flour, a teaspoon baking powder, 6oz/175g butter,

6oz/175g caster sugar, 2oz/55g finely chopped candied peel, a dessertspoon caraway seeds, three eggs beaten, milk.

Rub the butter into flour. Add the other ingredients and stir together before adding the eggs. Add sufficient milk to a soft drop texture. This amount is for an 8in/20cm cake tin, lined. It will need a good hour at 180°C/Regulo 4.

Another take on this cake is to use soft brown sugar, fresh lemon peel and juice instead of the candied, and half-and-half white and wholewheat flour. Grated nutmeg can also be added. Some cooks use more milk and not so many eggs.

Goosnargh cakes for Whitsuntide

... are more like biscuits than cakes. Again there are more variations than you could shake a duck at, and they can't even agree if it's Easter, Whitsun, Shrove Tuesday or leap-year muckspreading when you have them, but the basis is a shortbread mix with caraway seeds. Three of flour, one of butter, sugar as you like it, caraway seeds, possibly a few broken coriander seeds too, although it is not explained how coriander came to be traditional in Lancashire. Make the dough by kneading the butter and flour with a little sugar, add the seeds, roll out to your opinion of shortbread biscuit thickness, cut into rounds, sprinkle with more sugar, bake in a slow oven until pale gold, not brown.

Derbyshire wakes cakes are similar but with currants and grated lemon rind, sometimes with an egg and baking powder added. These are eaten during wakes week, a time of holidays and fun, the name coming from the custom of keeping watch over the dead with accompanying feasting.

Centaury, *Centaurium minus*

The fourth labour of Hercules/Heracles was to capture the Erymanthian Boar, a gigantic wild pig that ravaged wherever it liked because no one dared tackle it. On his way to complete the task, Heracles stopped off with a centaur called Pholus, a wise fellow of modest habits, which was a rare thing in a centaur for they were a race of beings, half man and half horse, known for their excesses in the wine and women department.

Anyway, Pholus broke out the wine for his Herculean guest and the smell attracted some of the other centaurs. A fight broke out. While Heracles was busy slaying centaurs, using arrows he had poisoned with the Hydra's gall during his second labour, one arrow accidentally fell on Pholus's hoof and he died instantly. Another arrow, stuck in the arm of a fleeing centaur, somehow transferred itself to the knee of the king of the centaurs, Cheiron, who was the only other nice one among them.

Heracles, distressed at this even worse accident, pulled out the arrow but the poison remained. Elsewhere, readers may see it given that the learned but wounded King Cheiron treated himself with the herb we now call centaury and so was cured. Alas, this was not so. The virtues of centaury were no match for the gall of the Hydra, and what would be? Cheiron could not be cured but, being immortal, he couldn't die either. That matter was later sorted by swapping mortality with Prometheus, and Heracles went off to catch the boar and take it to his master Eurystheus, who was always terrified when the hero was around and liked to go and hide in a bronze jar buried in the ground.

And that is how centaury got its name. A more prosaic version is simply that Cheiron, famous for his doctoring skills, was the centaur who discovered the powers of the herb.

The plant prefers dry and not too sunny spots and, sown in April, will produce a pretty display of pink-to-red flowers in July and August. It has various relatives in the gentian family, including the cornflower, that are more showy and so are more customarily seen in flower gardens. Common centaury is too bitter to be used in food and so has numerous virtues attributed to it, on the principle that anything that tastes awful must be good for you. It does act as a tonic and a mild laxative, and a stomach settler, taken as a tea made from the dried leaves and flower buds. One of its names is feverwort and that implies its reputation among 'country folk'.

Chervil, *Anthriscus cerefolium*

Not to be confused with sweet cicely, which is also called great, sweet and cow chervil, this is the culinary chervil not used for anything else. It looks like parsley, flowers in its second year, has leaves that turn pink in the autumn, and produces seeds that don't stay viable for long, so a good plan is to let it seed itself and gather ye flavoursome leaves while ye may, which can be only a few weeks after germination. Also like parsley, it is not so good when dried. The plant will grow more or less anywhere and is hardy.

Opposite page: Time was when parsley ruled, and no other herb found its way into ordinary kitchens apart from mint for mint sauce. In those days, a new detached house cost £1,000, a small family saloon car £125 and a good dinner could be had in a restaurant for half a crown. The ideal family consisted of a woman in a pinny laying the table, a small boy playing with Meccano on the carpet while his sister played with her dolls' house, and a man smoking a pipe while listening to the cricket on the wireless.

If the wife was serving fish for lunch, it would have parsley sauce, with fresh parsley from the garden or the market, the only herb she ever cooked with. Coriander? Never heard of it. Now we all know what coriander looks like and tastes like and, if we scattered a few seeds from the spice shop in our window boxes, we could have it all through summer.

Coriander, *Coriandrum sativum*

The delightful Frances Bardswell was a Victorian, writing soon after the old Queen died, well before the beginning of the First World War. This was an era when, some readers may be astounded to learn, Indian restaurants were unknown in this country. Officers and officials returning from imperial service in the subcontinent had been seduced by the food out there and they wanted *turrcarri*, but they couldn't go anywhere to get it. Veeraswamy, Britain's first Indian restaurant, wouldn't open until 1926. Miss Bardswell says 'A lady told me that a Spanish cook she had, positively refused to make a curry without Coriander seeds. They are perfectly round, like tiny balls.'

They are, indeed, Miss Bardswell, and that Spanish cook was absolutely right. Perhaps also she refused to serve a curry without scattering a few fresh coriander leaves on top which, of course, the gardener would have had to grow, it not being available in Waitrose at the time.

One problem with growing coriander, or cilantro as it is known in the New World, is that the seeds fall the moment they are ripe and so must be gathered slightly before. Also, for those lovers of fresh coriander, which must be everybody, the blasted plants will keep running to seed at the slightest change in the weather, or the phases of the moon, or something. At least, that is your correspondent's experience. Frequent sowings are therefore recommended.

Indian poached chicken with herbs

Cut a medium-sized chicken into eight pieces and poach in lightly salted water with a knob of butter and a few sage leaves added. Test after about forty-five minutes. When done, lift the chicken pieces out, drain, and put into a hot frying pan that has some butter sizzling in it. You are going to want about a cup of chicken stock so, if you have more than that, start reducing it.

To your buttered chicken add a handful of fresh coriander leaves and half a handful of chives, plus chilli to taste, fresh or ground. When all that is heated through, add half a cup of full-fat natural yoghurt and your reduced chicken stock. Simmer until the sauce is thick enough and serve.

Barbecued coriander aubergine

This is more of a method than a recipe. Beforehand, prepare the magic mixture, which is onion cooked in oil or butter but not browned, plus a good amount of broken coriander seed, a small amount of paprika, salt and a pinch or two of Chinese five-spice powder. This is based on an Indian dish; it's heresy to use five-spice, so let's call it fusion food.

On the barbecue, cook your aubergines, whole or halved as you like and depending on size, until tender. Scrape off the worst of the burnt bits and chop up. Throw your magic mixture into a frying pan on the barbie, add water if it looks dry, add your chopped aubergines and, when all is heated through, *la pièce de resistance*, a handful of chopped fresh coriander leaves.

Corn salad, *Valerianella locusta*

This hardy annual has been much promoted over the years as a winter and spring salad but it has never quite got off the ground, as it were, partly because you need to use the very young leaves which, being infants, are low growing and so offer you a soily and sandy harvest spattered by winter rains, to the point where you can't be bothered to pick them.

Should you be wishing to make a statement about intensively grown lettuce in the shops over winter, corn salad, also called lamb's lettuce, remains a way of doing it. It puts on growth in the winter and so wants a place as sunny and sheltered as possible. Sow in August and September, and again in March, and pull the little plants whole as you would lettuce thinnings.

Mrs Grieve says that corn salad 'was in request by country folk in former days as a spring medicine'. What the folk in question probably knew they wanted was something fresh and green, which tasted rather better than the stuff you could get from the hedgerow.

Cumin, *Cuminum cyminum*

The plant, which will grow well enough in the UK and ripen its seeds in a good summer, looks something like fennel. The seeds look like caraway, and the flavour is in that family too. The ancients thought cumin superior to both as a digestif but it is little used now by our herbalists.

It is paired with coriander in many Indian and other eastern dishes but seldom seen alone, although the seeds are sometimes used to flavour the bready pancakes called *dhosa*. There could be an ulterior motive for this because, in common with caraway, cumin was believed to be of use in cases of straying. Pigeon fanciers thought it helped the homing instinct. A lover, wishing to ensure the faithfulness of the beloved, might put cumin in the dhosas but would certainly expect cumin to be included in a magic potion, perhaps with caraway too in extreme instances.

> ### Seed potatoes
>
> This really quick dish can be served instead of rice with an Indian-style meal, or as well as. Have ready some cooked potatoes, cut into chunks. Heat butter or oil in a frying pan and add turmeric and salt. Stir, then add cumin seeds, coriander seeds, and black and white poppy seeds. When they start to pop, throw in your spuds, turn and stir to heat through and coat with the seeds. That's it.

Dill, *Peucedanum graveolens*

This one looks very like fennel but is a hardy annual. The leaves can be ready for use six or seven weeks after sowing but the seeds need a long summer to ripen, and it will grow more or less wherever you want it to grow. Dill has never really caught on in the UK, despite its great popularity in Scandinavia which is, after all, where a lot of us came from. There, pickling herring with dill is as natural as frying eggs with bacon is to us, and further east are millions of jars of small cucumbers in vinegar, sugar and dill.

Your correspondent had a Swedish friend who often bemoaned the lack of pickled herring in East Anglia. Pointing out the ease with which rollmops could be had produced only a wrinkling of the Nordic neb, and so, before discovering an excellent and widely available brand made in the Orkney Islands, which are pretty near Scandinavian anyway, said writer embarked on an experiment and found there wasn't really much to it.

You want herring fillets and salt to start with. Leave the former buried in the latter for a day or two in the fridge, then wash the fillets well. Wash them again. Taste a bit. If still too salty, steep in water for a while. Roll them up loosely, or leave them flat if you like, pack them in a jar or plastic container, add dill seeds, dill foliage and chopped onion as you see fit, pour on a mixture of half-and-half spirit vinegar and water, which you have sweetened to taste, and put in the fridge for a few days more.

The resulting delicacy, to be eaten as is, or with a herby tomato sauce, was almost fully approved by the Maid of Malmö as being good but not quite as good as she could buy over there, which seemed a bit of a cheek as she never did make them herself, whereas your brave correspondent had.

Good King Henry, *Chenopodium bonus henricus*

It's not *C. bonus Henricus rex* as you might expect, because it has nothing to do with any of our eight kings of that name, or their four French equivalents or any other of royal extraction, and is more commonly known in the wild as goosefoot. It's another of those plants that used to be cultivated as a green vegetable but fell out of favour when better things came along. Seed merchants keep trying to initiate a revival, as they do with corn salad, but Henry is really only worth growing as a curiosity. If you want a spinach substitute, spinach beet is far more productive, although Henry is less assertive on the palate.

If it is to be called good Henry without the king, to distinguish it from bad Henry and indifferent Henry, then nobody has yet identified any *malus henricus* or, for that matter, *quondam bonus et malus henricus*. It is native to northern climes and so it is faintly possible that is was named not for Henry/Henri/Heinrich, whose name means the prince of the house, but for Heimdall, Norse god, son of Odin, keeper of heaven's gates, guardian of the rainbow bridge. Heimdall is excellent at his watchman's job, ensuring no riffraff get in to Valhalla, because he can see in the dark and rarely sleeps, and then only for short naps. When he does nod off, he can still hear the grass-seed germinating and the wool growing on a lamb's back. And if the sheep developed a cough, what would be given to them? The root of good Henry, of course.

It's really a perennial but usually grown as a hardy annual for the young leaves, which are reputed to be a blessing in indigestion, and good for healing wounds. Gerard commends poultices of GKH for persistent sores, 'which they do scour and mundify'. Mundify is to cleanse. *The Classic Herb Garden*: a boon to Scrabble players.

Holy thistle, *Cnicus benedictus*

Called holy or blessed thistle, this relative of the asters had such a reputation in medieval times that it was prescribed against the plague. A clergyman called Thomas Brasbridge so believed in the plant's powers that he wrote a book about it, in 1578, in which he called the thistle the poor man's jewel. *Carduus* is the old Latin classification: *Poore Mans Jewell that is to say a Treatise of the Pestilence, unto which is annexed a declaration of the vertues of the hearbs Carduus Benedictus and Angelica which are very Medicinable, both against the Plague and also many other diseases.*

That something as important as a help against the plague should be so easily obtainable and yet so little known is the reason for the book. In its second edition, in 1592, he also states a simple truth which is sometimes forgotten these days. *For by heat and moisture, which proceed from the Sunne and the raine, all things growe upon the earth whereby man's life is maintained.*

Miss Sinclair Rohde holds that the plant is 'curiously attractive in appearance, with its long, decorative leaves and its pale yellow flowers, held in prickly involucres covered with brown bristles'. She could have put 'flowers wrapped in brown bristles', but she didn't. Sown in spring, it needs about two feet each way of space, and full sun. If it has to reach for the light it is liable to fall over, the burden of leaves and flowers being almost too much anyway for the slim stem.

No part of the plant is palatable for pleasure and so it must be grown for its looks and medicinal properties.

Marigold, *Calendula officinalis*

In warmer parts, marigolds will flower all year round, otherwise they are to be sown in the spring and will flower from June until the frost cuts them down. You only need do this once; *C. officinalis*, the old-fashioned pot marigold, not to be confused with the many fancy half-hardy annuals of flower displays, seeds itself with a will. It is called for the pot because, unlike most flowers, it was always a key ingredient in cooking. The dried flowers seem to have been used the way we use a pinch of mixed herbs or a stock cube, and the fresh flowers make a spectacular addition to salads. The leaves too are edible, at least the very young ones are.

It has many medicinal uses as well as culinary. Good old Culpeper says 'it is a herb of the Sun, and under Leo. A plaister made with the dry flowers in powder, hog's grease, turpentine and rosin, applied to the breast, strengthens and succours the heart infinitely in fevers, whether pestilential or not.' That may indeed be the case but neither Culpeper nor any of the other ancients, nor Mrs Grieve, make much of one virtue of marigold that is easily available today, in the modern equivalent of a hog's grease plaister, a tube of calendula ointment.

Possibly this is because minor matters such as dry and cracked skin were not considered sufficiently important to warrant mention, but your correspondent can vouch for the excellent ability of calendula to heal those painful cracks you get on either side of your thumb nail, which in the north are called keds, and which come when soft hands are made to do cold and/or manual work. It is also a very good anti-scratch. When you want to scratch something but you know you shouldn't because it will only make it worse, calendula ointment may soothe the irritation. A person of the author's acquaintance with mild psoriasis can confirm this point.

Milk thistle, *Silybum marianum*

This tall, handsome thistle is not a native of the British Isles and is quite rare here in the wild, preferring chalky soils by the sea. Where it does get a grip, as it might in a herb garden, it sows itself very freely. It's an escaper from medieval gardens where it was grown for both food and medicine, having been imported from the Mediterranean. The young leaves were eaten like spinach or raw in salads; older leaves were trimmed of their spines and boiled a bit longer. The stems, peeled and soaked for a while, otherwise they are rather bitter, were also a hot vegetable, as was the root.

Its medicinal properties are considered to be similar to those of the holy thistle (q.v.) and the old writers had plenty to say about it. Dioscorides said that a remedy could be made from the seeds that would cure 'infants that have their sinews drawn together, and for those that be bitten by serpents'. There's another reference to serpents in Anglo-Saxon literature: 'this wort if hung upon a man's neck it setteth snakes to flight'.

Anglo-Saxon herbalist: See ye, and wonder at it. With this wort upon my neck, it
setteth the snakes to flight.

Customer: But there are no snakes around here.

Anglo-Saxon herbalist: Exactly my point.

Orach, *Atriplex hortensis*

Also called arrach, and mountain spinach, this was the quick-growing green vegetable
of choice before there was very much choice. Proper spinach, spinach beet and so on
have consigned it to the garden of history, but it is still interesting to grow as a curiosity.
There are yellow/white and crimson forms as well as the standard green, which are
sometimes grown as ornamental plants but which are just as edible.

Sow in spring where it is to stand; do not transplant. It can grow quite tall but may
run to seed before full maturity. It's a goosefoot, a close relative of good Henry, and has
a similar if minor medicinal tradition though mainly seen as a vegetable.

Parsley, *Petroselinum crispum*

Mrs Grieve says 'There is an old superstition against transplanting parsley plants,' but
she doesn't say what it was. Miss Sinclair Rohde says that transplanting was thought to
be bad luck. Since parsley is a root vegetable that we grow for its leaves, like chard, and
since it is a biennial like its relative the parsnip, it will often respond to transplanting by
either dying or running quickly to fairly leafless seed, thus defeating its purpose, which
is indeed bad luck and hence, possibly, the superstition.

All the seed merchants offer several varieties of parsley, some have six or eight, and
there are dozens more on the register. Sowing parsley can be a frustrating business as it
takes so long to come up while weeds are faster, which is why many gardeners set aside
a small plot for the parsley and just let the crop get on with it, self-seeding one hopes
among a closely growing community, in which case it may decide to grow somewhere
else. Of course, if the parsley flourishes, that leaves the male gardener open to charges
of henpeckedness and increases the likelihood of his daughters remaining as spinsters.
Should the crop be poor, that means the grower is not an honest man.

Parsley, besides inflicting a no-win situation on male gardeners, also has a reputation as an
insect repellent, against fleas in the house and onion fly in the garden. Onions, while
growing, are held to repel the pest of another parsley relative, the carrot fly, so it may be
worth experimenting with sowings of parsley, spring onion and carrot for a fly-free summer.

Parsley's affinity with snails can be seen in restaurants, where parsley and garlic butter
is the most frequent accompaniment thereto, and in the cottages of French 'country
folk' who make an ointment of ground snails and parsley for treatment of scrofula –
the disease of swollen glands we call the king's evil.

Purslane, *Portulaca oleracea*

This hardy annual is quite succulent looking, sprawling about with red stems and fat leaves like the round ends of canoe paddles. It can be eaten raw or cooked; the mature stems make a decent pickle on their own and an interesting addition to piccalilli. It's not a great beauty but at least it's not just another anonymous, vaguely bitter, vaguely lettuce-tasting leaf in a bowl of anonymous leaves. It does stand out rather, in looks and in its bright, peppery flavour.

Soupe Bonne Femme

There are many, many variations on the theme of leek and potato soup. The Welsh have Cawl Cennin, which is made with the stock from boiling bacon. The Scots have Cock-a-Leekie, with chicken stock, and the French have Soupe Bonne Femme, also chicken stock. Most modern recipes for the latter are mere variations on a theme of plain leek and potato, as if Bonne Femme were no more than a hot version of Vichyssoise, but, like the other regional specialities, Welsh, Scots or whatever, its origins probably lie in the age before potatoes. Bonne Femme *vraiment* would have been thickened with oatmeal or barley, and would have had herbs as a much more important component than a simple garnish.

To an extent, the French goodwife soup would have used whatever vegetables came to hand, but sorrel and purslane are claimed to be the essentials that differentiate this soup from all others. If this is so, it must be from newly sown sorrel as previous years' perennial plants will be more or less finished before the annual purslane is up. Likewise, leeks will be finished and running to seed.

In any case, the Bonne Femme in question would have taken the stock from whichever bit of tough old meat she had been simmering, and added onions if she had any left, or onion greens from the new crop, and/or garlic, plus sorrel, purslane, probably cabbage, with oats or barley from the store to give it body.

We might look at this and think, as others have done before, that leeks and potatoes would be better, in which case, if you want sorrel and purslane you'll have to buy the leeks from the shop, so miss out the leeks, add carrots, and cabbage instead of the sorrel and purslane, think again and put the leeks back in, and you have Cawl Cennin.

Rampion, *Campanula rapunculus*

The wild rampion of Sussex, county flower thereof, is *Phyteuma orbiculare*, also a campanula family member but not one with a tradition of cultivation or herbal use. It has blue flowers something like a rather raggedy cornflower. The rampion available

How are the mighty fallen. Rampion, *Campanula rapunculus*, used to be in everyone's garden but now it is in hardly any. It's a salad, a cooked green veg, a root veg, and a medicine for the complexion and 'throte warts'. It has pretty flowers and it's easy to grow. It's lettuce, spinach, parsnip and floral decoration all in one plant but, like so many of the old favourites, not quite as good individually as its modern successors.

from specialist seed merchants and the one that used to be widely grown is *C. rapunculus*. It has crispy white roots that can be eaten raw or cooked, and leaves for the salad bowl or, later in the year, as a cooked green vegetable. Like all the tribe it has bell-like flowers, blue in this case and opened out starrily, but these are not to be permitted if you are looking for a good root harvest in the autumn.

Rapunzel, by the Brothers Grimm, reduced

Once upon a time, a couple longed for a child but couldn't have one. The woman, looking out over the garden belonging to the witch next door, saw a marvellous crop of rampion and persuaded hubby to go and nick some, otherwise he could expect her to die. Much against his better judgement, he did go and nick some, and she ate it in a salad and wanted more, because it was very nice and a kind of fertility treatment as well.

This time the witch, called Gothel, was waiting for him and she threatened to turn him into any terrible thing that he didn't want to be turned into. He explained the situation; she let him off and said he could have rampion *ad infinitum*, in return for the baby. He hesitated. She began casting a spell to turn him into a roll of loo paper. He agreed to her bargain.

When the wife was in labour, Gothel came in, disguised as the district nurse, and took the baby, calling it Rapunzel-Glockenblume, which is to say, Rampion. This baby grew into the most beautiful girl in the world so, naturally, the witch locked her in a room at the top of a tower. A handsome prince rode by, saw the witch at the bottom of the tower, and heard her calling 'Rapunzel, let down your hair.'

'Use the stairs, can't you?' replied the girl.

'As you very well know, dear, there are no stairs. Now, be a good girl and let down your hair.'

The prince saw the most beautiful face in the world appear at the window. A marvellous cascade of blond hair – the most beautiful hair in the world, in fact – tumbled down, and the witch climbed up it. 'I'm having a piece of that,' said the prince to himself. Next evening, he went to the tower and cried 'Rapunzel, let down your hair.' Down it came and up he went.

Even though she had never seen a man before, she agreed to marry him. So, how would she get out of her prison? Big problem. Princikins would have to come and see her every evening, and gradually bring with him the necessary components for a silk ladder, which she would hide from the wicked witch who would still be coming every afternoon. Rapunzel, the greenest herb in the garden, never asked princikins why he didn't bring a whole silk ladder in one go.

This went on for quite a while until the ladder was nearly finished and Rapunzel was indubitably with child. So happy was she that she quite forgot herself one afternoon, and asked the fat old witch why she was so heavy to pull up, compared to her princikins who had the correct body:mass ratio. At that, Gothel got proper blazing, cut off Rapunzel's hair, took her down the silk ladder in a fireman's lift and cast her into the desert. Climbing back up and pulling the ladder in after her, the witch tied Rapunzel's hair to the window sill, waited for the prince and tossed it down when he cried 'Rapunzel, let down your hair.' What a nasty surprise he had when he climbed in.

'She's dead!' screamed the witch. 'Gone! You'll never see her again! So, princikins, how do you like older women?'

He jumped out of the window and landed in a bush, which saved his life but blinded his eyes with thorns. He wandered about aimlessly, living off rough hawkbit and mugwort, until he heard a familiar voice. The voice said, 'About time, too. I've had to give birth to twins on my own, and now they're school age and I've got no money for uniforms.'

Rapunzel's tears washed the clouds from his eyes, so he could see to take her back to his homeland. His father, the king, made a great feast of welcome then died of joy, so the prince was king and Rapunzel was queen. They opened a successful hair-extension business, and they all lived happily ever after.

Rocket, *Hesperis matronalis*

The Latin name means 'lady of the evening', refering to the scent of rocket flowers which is only noticeable at the end of the day. Few gardeners grow it now for its flowers, which can be any shade between white and deep mauve and, not many years ago, very few grew it at all. Charlemagne and medieval gardeners viewed it as one of the basic essentials but it fell out of favour, only to become a fashionable salad ingredient, even to the extent of it appearing in bags in supermarkets and on the menu in sandwich shops. Its peppery taste does enliven a green salad, especially necessary with the increasing popularity of iceberg-type lettuces that really only offer texture rather than flavour.

It's a biennial, so salad seekers should treat it as an annual unless wishing to allow self-seeding, which it will do with great success. In the garden it also has the drawback of being attractive to cabbage whites. Its medicinal qualities are mostly redundant, it being regarded mainly as a cure for scurvy – a disease seldom encountered nowadays even by those who never eat rocket.

Summer savory, *Satureja hortensis*

This is a very good, general-purpose sweet herb, aromatic, easy to grow, and a handsome little bushy plant, dark green with small lilac flowers later on. You can use it wherever you might use any of the other sweet herbs, although it is more powerful than some and so should be employed with discretion. It is less assertive in taste than its winter sister and so more generally grown.

Modern herbalists don't give it much of a medicinal character, although our old friend Culpeper reckons it for all sorts. 'The juice dropped into the eyes removes dimness of sight if it proceed from thin humours distilled from the brain.' So, if your eyes are dim and you cannot see, and summer savory juice fails to sort it out, and you've tried yellow rattle, we can only assume that your affliction proceeds from a cause other than thin brain humours.

Chapter Four

Your Herb Garden

'The ideal way to make a herb garden would be to make little beds designed on decorative lines with perhaps a sundial and a seat. Such a garden could well be made near the kitchen quarters, particularly in any household where domestic help is employed. If so designed as to give privacy, and furnished as suggested with a seat, the herb garden would make an ideal resting place for the staff.'

M James, FRHS.

Nobody can tell you what to put in your herb garden, not even a Fellow of the Royal Horticultural Society. Only you know how much space you will allow, how enthusiastic you are, how much time you can give, and whether you lean towards the culinary, the

medicinal, the scented or the floral. You may like to mix herbs, as the word is usually understood, with 'proper' garden plants, like roses or buddleia. You may like the idea of wild herbs in a garden, or only privately educated ones, or a mixture of the two. Most people's idea of a wild garden is one left to revert as nature may or may not have intended, but you can guide a wild garden towards the prettier and/or more edible plants for example, or the more bee-loved, or the ones the ancients revered. Many plants we now consider wild-only were once cultivated, and seeds are widely available from specialist merchants.

What type of soil you have doesn't really matter a great deal. Some herbs will thrive better in this or that kind of ground but most will get along anywhere, provided they have some sunshine. A few like shade, a few like it damp – the mints for instance – and a few like it not too rich, but really there should not be many difficulties in that regard. You will still have plenty of choice, whatever your soil is like.

The Scented Garden

In the middle of the sixteenth century, Charles Estienne in his aforementioned *Agriculture et Maison Rustique* was recommending perfumed herbs, such as basil, chamomile, costmary, hyssop, lavender, lemon balm, marjoram, rosemary, sage and thyme, to make a scented garden. Another writer adds savory. In those days, such a thing was for the wealthy only. 'Country folk' might well appreciate the aromatic qualities of certain herbs but they were grown first and foremost for their usefulness.

We are more leisured now. If we have a garden, we can devote part of it to the pleasures of sound and scent. The golden rule to remember is that the scents of flowers come and go, while the scents of leaves remain. Of course, flowers give out all their scent freely; leaves usually need some encouragement, such as a little rub between finger and thumb. Even when dead and dry, leaves still have scent to offer. When flowers and warmth are long gone and winter's short, chill days are upon us, there are herbs to lift us with their aromas. As that romantic soul Percy Shelley put it, in his poem 'The Question':

> *I dreamed that, as I wandered by the way,*
> *Bare Winter suddenly was changed to Spring,*
> *And gentle odours led my steps astray.*

So, what do we need to plant so that our steps can be led astray? For their leaves, Frances Bardswell commends rosemary above all, and lavender, also bay, lemon balm, santolina – called cotton or French lavender – and southernwood. We could add eau-de-Cologne mint, and start thinking about flowers and plants such as hyssop and rue that you can strew on your conservatory floor next time you have friends round.

In the debate, if we are discussing a scented herb garden in the classic sense, when is a herb not a herb? Can you have a scented garden without sweet peas and roses? What about climbers and shrubs that would normally be considered part of the flower garden but are listed in the herbals as having useful attributes? Is honeysuckle a herb for our purpose, or jasmine?

We can condemn quite a few scented plants on this criterion – no herbal tradition – such as buddleia, night-scented stock and dianthus (pinks and carnations), and so many are the possibilities that if we are not very selective we won't be making a scented herb garden at all. So, let us start with a list that we can prune if we want, or, if very ambitious, to which we can add if we want, or if we feel tempted by Shelley's idea of straying.

Especially for the night: evening primrose, hesperis (sweet/garden rocket), honeysuckle, jasmine. In general: basil (*Ocimum basilicum*), bay (*Laurus nobilis*), beebalm/bergamot (*Monarda didyma*), lemon balm (*Melissa officinalis*), borage (*Borago officinalis*), burning bush (*Dictamnus albus*), catmint (*Nepeta sp.*), chamomile (*Anthemis nobilis*), coriander (*Coriandrum sativum*), false Solomon's seal (*Smilacina racemosa*), fennel

Charles Estienne, physician, royal printer and much else in sixteenth-century France, published a hugely popular book, called *The Country Farm* in English, which told you everything you needed to know about rural practices, including what to plant in your scented herb garden. One of his many, many other pieces of advice is to take some good wine and put to it equal quantities of rosemary flowers, cloves and ginger (presumably root ginger). Let all steep for eight days, then distil the result – which is illegal now, so a near equivalent would be to make some strong tea with the rosemary, cloves and ginger and mix that with brandy. The resulting 'water', it is promised, will cure stomach ache, kill worms, and make you thin if you are fat, and fat if you are thin, should you drink it with sugar.

(*Foeniculum vulgare*), heliotrope (*Heliotropium peruviana*), hyssop (*Hyssopus officinalis*), lavender (*Lavandula angustifolia*), pot marigold (*Calendula officinalis*), marjoram (*Origanum vulgare*), mint (*Mentha sp.*), myrtle in warm areas, rosemary (*Rosmarinus officinalis*), sage *greggii* and *grahamii*, southernwood, sweet pea (*Lathyrus odoratus*), tansy (*Tanacetum vulgare*), thyme (*Thymus spp.*), verbena (*Verbena spp.*), lemon verbena (*Aloysia triphylla/citriodora*), violet (*Viola odorata*), white balsam (*Gnaphalium polycephalum*), woodruff (*Galium odoratum*), wormwoods (*Artemisia spp.*).

But what about roses? Some herb-interested gardeners would not feel comfortable with the flash of hybrid tea and floribunda rose bushes in among all of this, nor might we want the ornate fancies of fashionable climbing varieties to make a hedge or barrier. Bearing in mind the words of our friend Shelley, further on in 'The Question' ...

And in the warm hedge grew lush eglantine,
Green cowbind and the moonlight-coloured may

... we might be inclined to follow the advice of Miss Sinclair Rohde again, on sweetbriars, also known as eglantine.

A clipped Sweet Briar hedge is a sight to make angels weep, but the bushes planted six feet apart and allowed to grow naturally soon attain a height of almost fourteen feet, throwing their graceful arching stems in all directions. In early spring, when the leaves are first put forth, they begin to exhale their fragrance; in June, when the long, slender branches are starred with their lovely flowers, they are exquisite; all through summer there is the pleasure of their scented foliage, a scent that is at its sweetest after a shower of rain, and in winter the myriads of brilliant red berries look like fairy lanterns. And unlike most Rose hips, those of Sweet Briar hang on till February and even March. Sweet Briars grow very quickly, and given sufficient space in a garden, they are naturally far finer than those that have to struggle for existence with other plants where they grow wild. A friend of mine who has a house aptly named Sweet Briars, planted a Sweet Briar hedge six years ago and put them six feet apart. The main stems are decidedly thicker than the average walking stick and the branches are quite fourteen feet high. Their fragrance fills the air for yards around.

The sweetbriar/eglantine here is *Rosa rubiginosa*. It has deep pink flowers, but that's not where the scent comes from. That special, appley smell is from the leaves, and especially so after rain. It tends to grow wild in limestone and chalky ground although may be spotted elsewhere. There is also the paler Lesser Sweetbriar, *R. micrantha*, which doesn't have such a powerful scent. Miss S R recommends planting lavender in front of sweetbriar, for the effect of the red hips against the grey of the lavender in winter, but she's not so keen on having any more *Rosaceae*:

If Roses be included in the herb garden they should be the old Roses. I have not in Plan I [see page 189] allotted any room to them, because I think that where there is enough space it is pleasanter to have a separate garden devoted to the old Roses. Opposite the Sweet Briar and Lavender entrance there might be a similar exit leading to the Old Rose garden, which should be laid out on the simplest lines.

Frances Bardswell would have you plant the moss rose, the damask rose and the cabbage rose in your herb garden, which latter bloom she says makes the best rosewater. It also was the traditional source of attar of roses in Europe, which we know these days as the essential oil, although in Asia they used *R. damascene*. By cabbage rose she means a variety of *R. centifolia*, a cross between the French or Provence rose, *R. gallica*, and the moss rose, also *R. centifolia*, which are still available from specialist growers.

The wild roses, such as the dog and the sweetbriar, grow only north of the equator, mostly in the temperate regions and have been the subject of gardeners' close attentions for many a year. With or without their help, various sports and mutations led to those moss roses, French roses, damasks and musks, but serious, hand-pollinated breeding didn't gain momentum until the early nineteenth century when the first hybrids appeared, giving long and more or less continuous flowering, leading over the next hundred years to the showy kinds of roses we know but may think inappropriate for a herb garden.

Growing fragrant plants demands some method of preserving that fragrance into the days when plants retreat but humans still must go about their business. Gathering and drying must be done just right if good results are to be achieved, and we shall not find anyone with more authority on the subject than Eleanour Sinclair Rohde:

> Bowls of fragrant pot-pourri are always a delight, especially in winter, when the sight and fragrance of them is a continual happy reminder of summer and sunny days in the garden.
>
> In most households there are treasured recipes for the making of pot-pourri, but a method a friend and I tried two years ago was so successful that I will describe it in detail. It is simple, it costs nothing beyond the flowers and scented leaves used, and the petals, etc., instead of being shrivelled, come out almost their original size. Consequently, instead of using a vast quantity of flowers and leaves, a small amount is sufficient.
>
> The method is based on one at least three hundred years old for drying Roses whole, and how much older I do not know, but I have never read of it in a modern book, and easy as it is, I had never seen it done before. It is described in that dainty little volume, *Delights for Ladies*, one of the most diminutive books of garden interest, and written by Sir Hugh Platt, one of Queen Elizabeth's courtiers. Every page in this tiny book – now extremely rare – is surrounded

with a design of the Rose of England, the Lily of France, and the Queen's initials, E.R.

And now for Sir Hugh Platt's method. Following his instructions we gathered the flowers – Roses, Carnations, Marigolds, etc., on a dry day, then we took shallow boxes (boxes in which notepaper is sold are admirable for the purpose) and put first a layer of sand, previously thoroughly dried. On this we laid the flowers, flat, and poured on to them more sand, taking care to keep the flowers open as much as possible and in their natural shape. Sir Hugh Platt directs placing the shallow boxes in 'some warme sunny place', but we placed them in the hot airing-cupboard, leaving the door slightly ajar. Of course the lids were not put on the boxes, for this would keep in the moisture. Then we forgot all about our experiment! About a fortnight later we remembered and hurried off to see the conditions of our dried flowers.

The result exceeded our expectations. For the dark red Rose petals we had gathered, instead of being shrivelled as in ordinary pot-pourri, were their proper shape and faded to a purplish red; the Clove Carnations were still whole and the

Thousands of varieties of rose, scented and non-scented, in almost every colour, have been bred from the few originals, and new ones are named every year. The wild dog rose is a very variable plant in itself, sometimes with pink and white flowers on the same bough, and has several close relatives liable to produce identical twins, making identification a job for the highly expert. We must believe that it has always been so and be glad that, every year, the simple wild flower shows us why an uncountable number of gardeners have been fascinated by that which we call a rose.

petals a lovely petunia colour; the Marigolds also whole and a brownish orange. A bowl full of these dried flowers is a charming and fragrant reminder of summer and far more attractive in appearance than most pot-pourris. Naturally the scent is not so strong as those in which various spices and gums are included. Personally, I prefer the faint, sweet fragrance of pot-pourri made only with flowers and leaves, such as sweet-scented Geranium leaves, to pot-pourris containing quantities of essential oils and so forth.

Pot-pourri made as described above cannot be left in open bowls indefinitely in a damp atmosphere, for the dried petals would absorb the moisture and decay. In a room where there are hot pipes any shelf or table near the heat is ideal. Failing this, it is as well to keep the bowl fairly near the fire.

A common mistake in making pot-pourri is to gather too many flowers at a time, for then they cannot be dried easily. It is better to gather small quantities, say once a week, and then store them as they are dried. Flowers and leaves should be gathered not merely on a dry day, but when there has been no rain for at least two days. Further, they must be gathered when the dew has quite dried off them. In a great many recipes the instruction is given to dry the petals in the sun, but I find that the best pot-pourri is made by drying in a very warm room in the shade. Full sunlight seems to destroy all but the strongest scents.

Thus far we have discussed the traditional scents employed in traditional ways but, without getting too far into the medicinal virtues, we can also consider those that have become more important with the rise of interest in aromatherapy. By this we mean the use of essential oils of certain plants, not so much to cure disease but to provide comfort, encouragement, stimulus and ease when we are in need of such. The argument is, if we can use the oils purchased in distilled form, we can use the plants as they are for similar effect.

Aromatherapy Herbs

You can make an essential oil from any plant, from lavender to cauliflower to Venus flytrap and back again, but only 160 or so oils are used in aromatherapy. Many of these duplicate each other, some are very expensive and difficult to obtain, most have more than one purpose, and some, if you were to believe all the claims made by their proponents, have so multifarious a range of marvellous properties that, as with Nicholas Culpeper's descriptions, you must ask why we need the rest or, indeed, any other form of therapy.

We can narrow the search. Going by popularity among the public, there is a top ten of essential oils sold in shops in the UK, and a top six of purposes for which they are bought.

Leaving aside those of the top ten oils extracted from the leaves, fruits and barks of trees, most of which are not a reasonable proposition for cultivation in Britain anyway, we are left with a top four aromatherapy herbs that are eminently suitable for the British garden: chamomile, geranium, lavender and rosemary. Not in the top ten oils because of high price but one we can certainly consider is rose. The good news is that all six of the big demands can be met with this small selection, and the demands are for:
• **relaxers:** aromas to help smooth away stresses and tensions in mind and muscle

- **revivers:** to help you pick yourself up, dust yourself off and start all over again
- **pain relievers:** for everyday aches, creaking joints and so on
- **skin improvers**
- **sleep inducers**
- **romance initiators/spice-uppers**

Beyond the chart-topping aromas we also have some good, solid players that are well worth your consideration: basil, clary (also called clary sage), fennel, ginger if you have a heated greenhouse or a warm conservatory, lemongrass if you have a greenhouse (likewise its relatives citronella, palmarosa and vetivert), marjoram, melissa (lemon balm), peppermint. There are scores more, mostly with parallel uses and some with hidden dangers, so this basic list might be worth sticking to.

You are almost certainly not going to try distilling essential oils. Besides needing a laboratory full of equipment, you would also need to grow on a commercial scale. One acre of lavender, for instance, might yield you a gallon and a half of lavender oil (about seven litres), more in a good year and with the most efficient methods. That's a terrible lot of oil if it's only for personal use but the point remains. What we are talking about here is deploying a modest supply of your home-grown plants for aromatherapy purposes using freely available technology such as the kettle, the airing cupboard and the hot bath – or you could buy the oil and use it beside your herb. This might be called cheating, or just sound practice, as when you make a curry with ground coriander in it, then sprinkle some fresh coriander on it.

Please note: essential oils can produce powerful reactions and some can be dangerous in certain circumstances, for example in pregnancy or where the 'patient' has high blood pressure. Simple use of leaves and flowers can only be a gentle form of aromatherapy, but please consult an authoritative guide before using any essential oil.

Chamomile, *Anthemis nobilis*

This is one of the more expensive oils, costing perhaps four times as much as basil or lavender, and so might be one of the more worthwhile plants to try growing. In aromatherapy it's seen as quite a versatile oil, as a relaxer and sleep inducer, a reliever of aches and pains, and good for your skin.

That cheery war-time slogan from HM Government, 'Keep Calm and Carry On', might well have said 'Keep Chamomile and Carry On', so highly recommended is this herb in the aromatherapy annals. If you are feeling stressed, emotional, upset, irritated or simply ill at ease with the way the world is treating you, chamomile flowers can help.

It can also come in usefully in cases of scratchy children, meaning children who have literally been scratched as well as those being bolshy at bath time. Chamomile is offered as an anti-inflammatory with mild analgesic properties, which extends its repertoire as an aid in tiredness after exertion. If you're too tired to sleep – it can happen – chamomile is, along with lavender, the most frequently quoted therapy.

Gardening in winter, walking in the rain, braving the salty breezes by the sea – these kinds of activities can make your skin sore; chamomile is your resource.

In aromatherapy, chamomile has a definite affinity with the feminine side. It may help with pre-menstrual tension; in perfumery, although not widely used, it is classified as a feminine scent. Chamomile flowers between the pillows may therefore be one girl's inducement to sleep while also being one boy's invitation to romance.

Geranium, *Pelargonium graveolens*

Like chamomile, geranium in aromatherapy is seen as skin-kindly, although more in cleansing mode for those problems that come with oily skin. Its main use, though, is in counterpoint to chamomile, being an uplifter and enlivener. When relaxation merges into doziness and the mood needs a kick and a spark, this is the one.

The leaves contain the magic ingredients, and they are not so much keep calm and carry on as get off your behind and up and at 'em. Sometimes, when the day has dealt you savage blows, the land of Nod and chamomile are indicated. Other times, even though you want to pull the duvet over your head, you absolutely must remember those famous men, who had to fall to rise again. Send for the geranium.

Perfumiers classify geranium as attracting both male and female, and some enthusiasts are certain it can be a positive force when you need to put another log on the fire of love. In any case, its bright and lively smell must be for the good when such matters arise.

Lavender, *Lavendula angustifolia*

If you were to grow only one plant for aromatherapy, this would be it. It has no claims made for it as an aphrodisiac but its list of virtues is pretty comprehensive otherwise.

Medicinal uses are dealt with elsewhere in the book. Here we shall concentrate on lavender's special qualities as a mediator in the battle of the spirits. Let us suppose that a sequence of events, such as the car not starting, the supper burning, the cat peeing on the carpet, and half an hour on the phone spent pressing two for this and three for that, has brought about in you a case of the screaming habdabs. The aroma of lavender offers you a return to normality, a soothing, wash-your-cares-away kind of correction of your spiritual imbalance.

Or, let us suppose a different series of impacts on your good nature. The gas bill has arrived and it is horrendous, you've had a stupid row with your significant other or best friend over nothing, and your tomato plants have all got blossom-end rot. Obstacles and dark clouds are in your way but lavender can dispel them. It's going to be a bright, bright sunshiny day.

Lavender has this rare facility for bringing you up when you're down, and for gathering you safely in when you think that going to pieces is the easy option. A small muslin pouch of lavender flowers under the pillow should help you sleep. If it doesn't, people have been making a lavender mistake for thousands of years. A stronger dose, such as might be had by inhaling the steam from a bowl of lavender 'tea', can have the opposite effect and send you out into the world refreshed and revitalised, although, of course, smelling of lavender. It will help keep the midges away too.

Rosemary, *Rosmarinus officinalis*

One therapeutic use of rosemary's aroma is to keep witches away. This writer's garden has several rosemary bushes and no witch has ever been seen, so it must work. It also improves memory, so it's a good idea to have vases of rosemary all over the house, then, when you go into any room, you can sniff the rosemary and remember why it was that you came into that room in the first place.

Regardless of such matters, peoples of the Mediterranean, where rosemary is native, have always used the flowering sprigs for their cleansing powers, both in body and mind. The smell of rosemary is like a break in the clouds; it sharpens, enlivens and brings a smile.

Rose, *Rosacea spp.*

There are thousands of different roses, some with no smell, some with lots of smell, some with smells that are floral but not really rosy. The types used by the perfume industry to make their highly specialised oils are mostly in the damask rose (*Rosa damascene*) and cabbage rose (*R. centifolia*) families, and the aromatherapist's oil is usually from the damask, but you should choose the ones you like best or think will work the best, depending on the purpose you have in mind.

Although rose is classified as a good multi-purpose scent like lavender, most people will think of it in romantic terms. It is a very feminine aroma and has been used for eons to attract those who, in touch with their masculine side, would like to meet those who would be interested in having their feminine side touched. When Marlene Dietrich was falling in love again, she had men clustering to her like moths around a flame. Possibly she was wearing a rose-based perfume.

Rose is also given as good for the skin, in care and repair, and as an antiseptic, astringent, and uplifting tonic.

Basil, *Ocymum basilium*

The aroma of this warm-climate relative of the mints and the thymes is seen as a stimulant, a cooling restorative, a purifier and air freshener.

Clary, *Salvia sclarea*

If you want to know what effect clary might have on you, think about your reaction to a glass of wine or two. A drink can make some folk cheery and some morose, some dozy and some amorous. In most cases, it seems to be able to soothe and uplift simultaneously.

In perfumery, clary is mostly used in men's products although it is classed as both a male and female fragrance, so you can make what you like of that.

Fennel, *Foeniculum vulgare*

In ancient times you might have believed that inhaling the scent of sweet fennel would give you mental strength in dire circumstances, and give you long life. You might also have strewn the plant around to ward off the bogeyman.

Its use as a digestif is covered elsewhere in this book. Breathing in the steam from a hot decoction should help you look on the bright side of life and may even, like the famous sweet called Tunes, help you breathe more easily, although the manufacturers of Tunes are not allowed to say that any more.

Ginger, *Zingiber officinale*

Therapists use the oil for tired and aching bodies. To say that the aroma of ginger is regarded as warming and enlivening will come as no surprise and, for lovers, these effects may be deployed to advantage.

You can grow your own ginger fairly simply if you have a heated greenhouse or a warm conservatory. First step is to pop down to the greengrocers sometime in February or early March and buy the freshest looking set of ginger fingers that have little extra cones on the end. These are your budding shoots. Ideally, there will be at least two inches of finger behind each bud.

Separate the fingers, with a knife if necessary. One-third fill eight-inch pots with soil or a good fertile compost, stand a finger in each, bud upwards, fill the pots and firm. It's hot and wet where ginger normally grows, so you need to water regularly, also spray with warm water twice a day, and don't expect any action below 28°C. Replant in larger pots as you see fit and every couple of weeks give a general-purpose feed.

Come September, you need to imitate the plant's natural dry season. Gradually cut down on the watering and eventually let the pots dry out entirely. Now, with any luck, you will have ginger. Don't bother trying to keep a plant back to provide rhizomes for next year. It will almost certainly die in our short winter days.

Lemongrass, *Cymbopogon citrates*

The species of lemongrass mostly used for essential oil extraction, because it is more useful medicinally, is *C. flexuosus*, also called East Indian lemongrass, while the one you see in the shops for cooking will most likely be *C. citrates*, also called West Indian.

The aroma is anathema to insects but good for clearing the woozy minds of humans, who may also find it has a sedative effect. On the other hand, its masculine, deodorising qualities may prove attractive.

Lemongrass has several relatives with similar properties: citronella, *C. nardus*, is perhaps more powerful against insects and as a deodorant; palmarosa, *C. martini*, is valued as an appetiser and tonic; vetivert, *Vetiveria zizanioides*, is stronger as an oil on troubled waters.

For growing your own, the lemongrass that you buy in the shop could easily be dry beyond redemption. You must pick stalks that still have life in them and, ideally, have a few bits of root stubble left. Peel away any dead matter and stand your stalks in a jar of water, somewhere light and warm. When you have visible roots, plant each stalk – white part submerged – in an eight-inch pot and keep moist but not sodden. In a warm British summer it will thrive by the edge of your garden pond but mature plants, which multiply rather like a Welsh onion, will not stand our winters. To harvest, grip a stalk at soil level and pull away.

Marjoram, *Origanum majorana*

The aroma of sweet marjoram is recommended for insomnia and is said to be a help to those in a poor emotional state, such as one recently bereaved. It is supposed to have featured in long-ago weddings although, curiously, it was also prescribed for sexual over heating and, like hops, was regarded in certain quarters as a turn-off.

Melissa, *Melissa officinalis*

More usually known as lemon balm, this is the fragrant herb that cheers. Like most things lemony, the aroma is masculine, lively, and a help if it's raining in your heart. Although it can be an aid in skin complaints, by far its most frequent therapeutic use is as a general tonic, perhaps especially effective for those who feel dazed and confused.

Peppermint, *Mentha piperita*

This is the scent that cuts through the fog, clears the channels, cools and invigorates. Trouble is, every time you smell it you think 'toothpaste' and 'chewing gum'.

Yes, you can eat it, but you wouldn't pick primroses from the wild. You might not realise that young hogweed is actually quite nice in a salad.

Chapter Five

Can You Eat It?

This chapter is about plants that we wouldn't normally consider to be part of our diet, mostly because we can't be bothered with foraging any more, or because there are more refined and more easily available alternatives, or because we are conditioned to think of the plant in question as a weed.

As we all know, a weed is a plant in the wrong place. In the right place, it's a herb. Even so, the majority of edible wild herbs, of which there are many, are not really worth the trouble except as an interesting experiment. They tend not to have big leaves like spinach beet or big hearts like lettuce or big roots like parsnips, and they can taste too bitter, but some are common and/or easily grown and moderately useful, especially in spring when there may not be so much fresh stuff in your garden. These are they.

With a name like black medick, this diminutive relation of alfalfa must, you would think, figure strongly in the herbal annals. Not so. You can eat *Medicago lupulina*, just about, and that's all. The name is from the Greek, meaning the grass that grows in Media, which, as every school child used to know, was where the Medes came from, as in the Medes and the Persians. Modern Media is in north-west Iran, below the mountains of Kurdistan, but their grass is everywhere.

Yes, you can, but you might not want to. Curled dock, *Rumex crispus*, is bitter when mature but fine when it's very young like this, in early spring. Try it in a ham omelette. *Rumex alpines*, patience dock also called herb patience and, more usually, monk's rhubarb, is another edible dock but rarer, with large, heart-shaped leaves. Its common name derives from it having been grown widely as a green vegetable by the monastic orders and used by them as a laxative.

The rhizomes of the bulrush or reedmace, *Typha latifolia*, are a carbohydrate-rich if rather fibrous food for winter. Be careful, though, because the cooked rooty bits have the same reputation as dandelions. An ointment for burns and scalds can also be made from the same part.

Alexanders, *Smyrnium olusatrum*

Generally described as liking coastal areas, this large and abundant herb is marching inland and is much more common than it was only a few years ago. It's not a native, having been imported as a garden vegetable in Roman times or before, but it has certainly fitted in well.

It's early, surfacing even in January and February, and its green-yellow flowers come in April. Looking like a squatter, glossier version of hemlock, to which it is related, alexanders offers many things but not a means of Socratic self-termination. Hemlock, by the way, grows large at six or seven feet and has spotty stems and a horrible smell when you crush or break it. Beware.

Young alexanders leaves and flower buds go in salads but the real prize is the stem. Near the bottom of the plant you should be able to find a length of stem that is paler, less green than the rest. This is the part you want. Steam a bundle of these stems and, with butter or mayo, you have asparagus. Well, sort of.

Alexanders, also called horse parsley, was always considered a pot herb until better green things came along. It was known as black lovage by the old herbalists because the fruits turn almost black as they ripen. It is a relative of garden lovage and the wild scots or sea lovage, being in the great *Umbelliferae* tribe, but not an especially close one.

Burdock is probably not a plant you would want in your herb garden, unless you had a great deal of space and were much inclined to the wild side. Of course, really wild gardens can attract really wild life, in which case the advice of Nicholas Culpeper might be followed, because 'a juice of the leaves or rather the roots themselves given to drink with old wine doth wonderfully help the biting of any serpents'.

Burdock, *Arctium spp.*

There are three burdocks: the Great, *Arctium lappa*, the Common, *A. pubens*, and the Lesser, *A. minus*. All have large leaves at the bottom of a strongly growing plant three or four feet high, smaller leaves near the top, and thistly flower heads that turn into those brown burs that catch in clothing and dogs' coats.

The stems when young can be peeled and what's left cooked in your preferred manner, giving you a soft vegetable tasting vaguely of aniseed. The roots, dried and ground, can be used with dandelion roots to make a variation on the uncaf coffee substitute or the famous soft drink, although it won't turn out much like the commercial dandelion-and-burdock pop you drank in your youth, which had nothing of either plant in it.

Probably the nearest you will get to real dandelion and burdock, whatever that is, would be by following the nettle beer recipe (see page 181) and adding a few star anise and/or pieces of liquorice root.

The brave little chickweed's tiny white flowers push up between red dead and stinging nettles.

Chickweed, *Stellaria media*

This is another disparaged and persistent weed, executed by modern gardeners everywhere although cultivated enthusiastically in medieval plots. Chickweed's tiny leaves are far too small to pick, so lift the whole plant, trim off the roots if you can be bothered, wash thoroughly and stir fry.

Use it raw, anywhere you would use lettuce or cress. It's very good in a Yorkshire salad, which is the same as a Greek salad but with Wensleydale instead of feta and silverskin pickled onions instead of olives.

Cow parsley, *Anthriscus sylvestris*

If alexanders is on the march, cow parsley seems to be in retreat. In the late spring, every lane and byway used to host waving oceans of the white flowers of cow parsley, but it's still common enough. Its virtues lie in sparing use as a flavouring, not in salads. It is nothing like parsley but a lot like chervil, although sharper, so, use with tomato salads, omelette *aux fines herbes*, new potatoes, shellfish and so on.

Comfrey, dandelion, nettle, dock – a veritable wild pantry. Don't bother with the celandine.

Beware of hemlock again but also of a feeble-looking, smaller, weedier, smellier version called fool's parsley that has danglers under its flowers. If in doubt, don't pick.

Dandelion, *Taraxacum officinale*

This writer, in younger and less knowledgeable days, was once amazed by a kindly neighbour bringing around a tray of dandelion seedlings. She grew them for salads. After a gentle but firm rejection, she went home while the said writer got out his hoe and set about the massacre of the many innocent young dandelions in his vegetable plot.

Had he known better, he might have planted a few in rich soil and have been equally amazed at the size they can grow to, and the continuous production of leaves except in the very coldest weather. The neighbour might have told him that he could blanch the leaves with an upturned bucket if he wanted, or cook them like spinach. Mostly, though, you would use the green part of the leaf, not so much the stalk, as a sharpish salading. You can also chop them fine and use where you might otherwise have sorrel or chives.

There is a French dish called *pissenlit au lard* which, amusingly, translates literally as 'wet-in-the-bed at the bacon'. They could just as easily call it *dent-de-lion au lard*, lion's

Young dandelion leaves are perfectly good to eat. So are young cow parsley leaves, and not only for rabbits.

tooth at the bacon, but they prefer to refer to the plant's diuretic reputation.

Anyway, to make the dish you fry small pieces of bacon until crisp, then scatter on a bed of dandelion leaves that have been sprinkled with a dressing. A more complex and hearty recipe comes from the Ardennes, for *salade au lard*, which is served traditionally during the grape harvest. This features a quick fizz on the stove for the dandelion leaves, finely chopped (or not, depending on which village you come from) in a little olive oil with some minced shallot. You add slices of cooked potato (cooked in their skins, or not, depending etc.) and your crispy bacon (smoked or not, lean or fatty, depending again) and toss in a dressing when cool, or just in vinegar and salt. You can use a curly endive (*salade frisée*) instead of the dandelions, but only if you come from Paris.

Dandelion roots make a good and much, much cheaper substitute for decaf coffee. You make an autumn harvest, digging up the roots when they are in their prime, and wash your crop thoroughly. Dry the roots, in the sun if there is any, otherwise in the airing cupboard or similar, then roast them brown and snappable. Grind and use as coffee.

The fresh root, thinly sliced but not peeled, can also be part of your stir fry although the slices will benefit from going in first or being steamed a little. Apparently they use it so in Japan.

Fat hen, or white goosefoot, also called dirty dick for its propensity for growing on muck heaps, is a nutritious plant that helped to sustain the human race long before anyone did any gardening. It is a close relative of good king Henry, which is also sometimes called fat hen because the two of them were thought to make excellent chicken browsing.

Dandelion tea, taken morning and night, is given as a benefit to sufferers from arthritis and rheumatism. Fresh dandelion leaves are also supposed to stimulate the metabolism and generally act as a tonic, so what we need is a dandelion guru to design and promote the Dandelion Diet.

There are quite a few dandelion-looking plants that also have edible leaves, for instance the various hawksbills, catsears and hawkbits, all *Compositae* family and useful as salad lifters if not as the main ingredient. One that swaps well with dandelion is corn sowthistle, if you can be patient enough to snip off the prickles from the edges of the leaves.

Fat hen, *Chenopodium album*

All gardeners will know this one as a weed that seems to appear five minutes after the soil has been turned over. Prehistoric man knew it as a valuable and nutritious food and so did all manner of folk, including country folk, until spinach and similar vegetables made it redundant.

Next time you see it in your vegetable patch, which is to say next time you look at your vegetable patch, let some grow and have your revenge by serving it as steamed greens.

Garlic

Two quite different and unrelated plants offer a garlic flavouring in their leaves. Hedge garlic, *Alliaria petiolata*, aka garlic mustard, Jack-by-the-hedge etc., looks something like lemon balm with bigger, ragged-edged leaves. It's one of the earliest wild herbs. It makes a good addition to a plain green salad, or you can make a sauce with it as you would with mint.

The stronger one we normally call wild garlic, *Allium ursinum*, aka ramsons, has a powerful smell that can often be noticed from quite a distance. The spearhead-shaped, glossy leaves are very garlicky used raw but soon lose their pungency in the pan. A few seconds' acquaintance with boiling water followed by rinsing in cold may be your best compromise.

Wild garlic is plentiful in woodland but not in all districts. If you'd rather grow your own, gather a mature seed head in early summer, then dry and sow in autumn in a shady part. It won't bulb up like tame garlic but is well worth it for the leaves alone, and the flowers look pretty in salads too.

Hedge garlic, called Jack-by-the-hedge, offers a mildly garlicky addition to a salad or a change from mint sauce.

Good king Henry, *Chenopodium bonus henricus*

In the same family as the various goosefoots, good king Henry is a herb that has gone through all the stages of popularity and back again. Like fat hen it was a prehistoric staple, then it was kept going as a minority-interest garden plant, then it fell out of favour entirely and then, like rocket, has reclaimed its place as a cultivated food with packets of seeds widely available.

The man on the galloping horse would be hard put to distinguish good Henry from fat hen, and only the most studious of vegans would be able to tell them apart as food.

Goosegrass, *Galium aparine*

Gathered intentionally or unintentionally, and before the little green balls of seed appear, this herbal Velcro can be rendered more or less edible by giving it the spinach treatment. Later in the year, you can add the seeds to your dandelion and burdock coffee mixture.

Not to everyone's taste but plentiful, and so guilt-free to gather, hedge garlic can go in the salad early in the year, and young goosegrass makes an acceptable spinach substitute.

Ground elder, *Aegopodium podagraria*

More good news for the gardener. The most hated weed of all can be eaten. Time was when people grew it on purpose and allowed it to mature, when it has heads of small white flowers something like tree elder that turn into seedpods. Now, surely, in the garden it can only be a by-product of some hefty clearance work because nobody would want to leave a scrap of root behind if it could be helped.

Cook it like spinach, that is, like most of these green, unconsidered trifles, with very little water, or none and a knob of butter or a slurp of oil, and for only a few minutes.

Himalayan balsam, *Impatiens glandulifera*

This Asian version of busy Lizzie gone crackers has colonised so many slow-flowing streams, especially in southern districts, that it has eliminated almost everything around it. Spectacular though it may be in flower, it is so invasive as to justify mass harvesting for the pot. The young leaves and stems can be cooked as a vegetable, and the seeds can also be used where you might otherwise have lentils or dhall. Howsomever, take care

Eat with your eyes. Dead-nettles make a pretty addition to the salad bowl.

when gathering seeds. If the pods are mature they are liable to explode, scattering their cargo to the four winds, which rather defeats the controlling aspect of the harvest.

Nettles

Probably the most common herb of all, the stinging nettle, *Urtica dioica*, is good to eat when young but, considering its ability to inflict damage, surprisingly boring when cooked. Only masochists would eat it raw. The white and the red dead-nettle, *Lamium album* and *L. purpureum*, are all right raw or cooked.

There are dozens of nettle recipes but they have one thing in common: the inclusion of flavoursome ingredients to help the plainness of nettle on its way. Do not try stinging nettle when mature. It tastes pretty awful although it relieves constipation.

You can use any and all of the nettles, plus young non-giant hogweed, to make Wild

Some aficionados of the stinging nettle would say it is as good to eat as spinach. Most people would say good, but not that good.

Herb Aloo. Take equal quantities by weight of new potatoes, wild greenery and sliced onion, let us say a pound of each, or 450 grams. That's a lot of nettles, but they go to nothing in the cooking. Boil the spuds *al dente*. Sweat the onions in plenty of butter, adding garlic (could be wild) as you like, half a teaspoon each of ground coriander, ginger, paprika and salt, and three or four cardamoms. Add chilli or cayenne also, if you want. Throw in the potatoes and the greenery, and stir furiously over a medium heat until the nettles and so on have wilted and everything is hot. Add some yoghurt to make a sauce.

Ox-eye daisy, *Chrysanthemum leucanthemum*

Now much more common than it used to be, owing to its last-man-standing persistence in commercial wild flower sowings, this easy plant's roots are said to make a salading.

The relatively dainty red dead-nettle is surrounded by the bullying hogweed or cow parsnip, *Heracleum sphondylium*, which itself is fine to eat when young. Beware of the very large relative, the poisonous giant hogweed, *H. mantegazzianum*, with red-spotted stems up to ten feet high and much larger leaves, less common and very noticeable.

They are also said in folklore to stunt your growth, so possibly the best use for them is as rhyming slang for boots.

Sweet galingale, *Cyperus longus*

Historically a plant of southern England, growing beside ponds and ditches as the family tends to do, this particular sedge has an aromatic root which, dried and powdered or sliced fresh, can be used where a milder version of ginger would be appreciated. It is not a common plant but can be grown from seed should you find some, and it's increasingly popular as a plant for park lakes as global warming allows it to move northwards.

Three-cornered leek, *Allium triquetrum*

Spreading from the south west of England, this garlic–chives-flavoured plant may soon be growing on a verge near you. It looks like an especially lush, long, green kind of grass

Yet another weed we used to feed on, the smooth or common sow thistle, *Sonchus oleraceus*, is nowadays regarded as fit only for rabbits. The ancient Greeks thought it food fit for heroes. Cook the leaves like spinach and see for yourself.

but the blades have a distinctive ridge down the middle and a strong garlic smell when crushed. Use as you would chives.

Water mint, *Mentha aquatic*

The Reverend Keble Martin lists eleven varieties of the family *Menthae* as growing wild in Britain, including corn, spear, pepper, horse and French, but the mint of the water is the most useful in the kitchen, and it's common everywhere. It's easy to recognise: it looks like mint, it grows near water and, uniquely for a mint, it has its lilac-ish coloured flowers all at the top of the stem. Use as you would garden mint.

Alkanet

Chapter Six

Herbs for Health

The green or evergreen alkanet, *Pentaglottis sempervirens*, has flowers of a startling blue and looks well in any garden although it needs discipline. It's not a British native but a naturalised import for cultivation, from warmer parts, probably Spain, and now grows wild anywhere. The alkanets are borage family and offer a red-orange dye from their roots; the name comes from the Arabic *al-hinna*, their word for the Egyptian privet from which henna proper is made.

According to our friend Culpeper, alkanet is not just a pretty flower, for it 'strengthens the back, and easeth the pains thereof. It helps bruises and falls, and is as gallant a remedy to drive out the smallpox and measles as any is; an ointment made of it is excellent for green wounds, pricks or thrusts.'

Tea can be made from its leaf buds and a dye from its flowers, but it has no role whatever as a medicinal herb, other than that of a work of nature's art. Look at it and marvel, usually on heathland near the sea. On a fine day with a sea breeze, a sight like this must be as good for you as any medicine. This gorse grows near Dunwich, Suffolk.

The family *Caryophyllaceae* includes the pinks, sweet William and a whole load of mouse-ears, stitchworts, and chickweed, not to forget the Nottingham catchfly. Here we have the very familiar red campion, *Silene dioica*, and ragged robin, *Lychnis floscuculi*, which may well have similar virtues to their relation soapwort which, Mrs Grieve tells us, is a good cure for old venereal complaints, especially where mercury has failed.

The yellow rattle, *Rhinanthus minor*, lives partly off the roots of the grasses among which it grows, like eyebright, and was held to have similar properties to that other semi-parasite. The rattle is the seed pod and, says Culpeper, 'the whole seed being put into the eyes draweth forth any skin, dimness or film from the sight without trouble or pain'. Gather seeds in late summer from the wild or buy from a wild-flower seed supplier. Rather than put it in your eyes, rake it into your wild flower meadow. It encourages other flowers by restraining the more rapacious grasses.

The hawksbeards are best told from each other by their leaves, as the flowers of the stinking, bristly, smooth, French, rough, soft and marsh hawksbeards are very similar to each other and to this one, which is the beaked hawksbeard, *Crepis vesicaria*. The hawkweeds, *Hieracium spp.*, are even more difficult, and you also have the hawkbits for good measure. All are dandelion-type plants in the great *Compositae* tribe and are generally treated as one by the herbalists. Dioscorides says they are drying and binding, good for the heat of the stomach and gnawings therein. Beaked hawksbeard does have edible leaves if you are ready to spend the time picking them, otherwise its main use is as a food plant for butterflies and bees.

It looks like a thistle but really it's an aster. The holy or blessed thistle is an annual, not a perennial, and, unlike any other member of the aster family, once had a reputation for curing just about everything, including the plague. The plague isn't around much any more, but large doses of the dried herb will act as a strong emetic and thus make you vomit, 'with little pain or inconvenience', as Mrs Grieve puts it. Smaller doses are said to increase the flow of milk in nursing mothers and various old authorities say it can cure deafness and strengthen the memory.

Any advertising agency would surely have been eager to hire William Turner as a copywriter. Here he is, in his *New Herball*, 1568, foreshadowing the television commercial voice-over: 'There is nothing better for the canker and old rotten and festering sores than the leaves, juice, broth, powder and water of Carduus benedictus.' It does just what it says on the tin.

Of course, old Nick Culpeper has to spoil it all with his nonsense: 'It is a herb of Mars, and under the sign of Aries. The continual drinking the decoction of it helps red faces, tetters and ringworm, because Mars causeth them.' We must hasten to state that we are talking here of the planet Mars and not of the confection of that name. A tetter, by the way, can be any of several skin diseases including impetigo, eczema, psoriasis and herpes. There's another one for our Scrabble players.

Furthermore, says Culpeper, 'By Antypathy to other planets: it cures the French Pox by Antypathy to Venus who governs it.' French or Spanish Pox was the name euphemistically given to syphilis, which is rarely contracted while playing Scrabble.

The vetches – this is bush vetch, *Vicia sepium* – have traditionally been seen more as food than as medicine and seem to have no place in herbal lore. However, recent research indicates that they may be an important source of phenolic compounds with high antioxidant activity, which is another way of saying that there may be a possibility of medicinal uses against heart disease and other ailments. While it is quite clear that phenolic compounds are essential in many plants, their role in human biology is more controversial.

Creeping cinquefoil, *Potentilla reptans*, also called five-leaf grass, has been used in medicine since the earliest times. Good old Dioscorides commended it for fevers, while Culpeper gives it for jaundice, toothache, coughs, shingles, sciatica and 'hurts by blows'. Modern herbalists might prescribe it for that embarrassing condition we call the squits.

Medicinally, coriander seed is a mild digestif but has mainly been used as an aromatic disguise for less agreeable dosings. In the days when children were satisfied with plainer sweets than now, comfits were made by coating coriander seeds in sugar. People still chew the seeds for their flavour and for sweetening the breath, although governments warn officially that too much can have a narcotic effect. How much is too much, we are not permitted to know.

The seeds of cumin, very similar to those of caraway, were considered superior by the ancients and were widely prescribed for those discomforts occurring in that part of the system concerned with food and drink processing. 'A corrective for the flatulency of languid digestion' is how Mrs Grieve puts it, and for 'pains in the side caused by the sluggish congestion of indolent parts'. Meals at Indian restaurants often contain considerable amounts of cumin.

There are several woundworts which, like woad, were prescribed for the treatment of cuts and bruises. This is hedge or wood woundwort, *Stachys sylvatica*, with flowers varying from deep crimson to purple and always one of our finest in late May and early June. To prove that beauty is only skin deep, it smells rather unpleasant, especially when crushed. Toads are said to prefer it to other flowers as a parasol.

Nodding violets, *Viola odorata*, nod not so much as they did, and so we must not follow the ancients in their pursuit of the sweet smell of the flower and the beneficial qualities of the leaves, which were used for bruises, swellings and other superficial damage. The old recipe added three dozen leaves to two ounces of clarified lard, cooked together in a slow oven or a bain Marie until a green, lardy kind of paste resulted. The vegetation was strained from it while hot, and the impregnated fat used as an ointment when cool.

The leaves of the bog violet, like those of its land-based and more fragrant relative, will, according to the ancients, comfort the heart and assuage the pains of the head.

There are many species of corydalis, all credited with abilities in pain relief and relaxation of nervous disorders, but, being slightly toxic, considered unsuitable for pregnant and nursing women. This is climbing corydalis, *Corydalis claviculata*, which likes sandy heathlands and places where bracken grows.

The small-flowered cranesbill, *Geranium pusillum*, has all the qualities of the other cranesbills but it is, as its Latin name says, very small and insignificant, although possibly not to piles sufferers.

The cranesbill family, *Geranium spp.*, are generally valued for the root, which is rich in tannins. The uses are mainly among the more unpleasant of human ailments, including diarrhoea and piles, which perhaps says something about the professional dedication, or lack of artistic appreciation, of the early herbalists. Confronted with such beauty as here, a specimen of hedgerow or Pyrenean cranesbill, *G. pyrenaicum*, the village wise-woman would see, not a glory of nature, but something to dig up to make a cure for her customers' haemorrhoids.

Comfrey growing wild, as here, seems generally to be in advance of the stuff in your garden, possibly because it has chosen its ideal spot. As the Ministry said in 1941, comfrey, though not officially included in the British Pharmacopoeia, is widely used in some country districts, particularly Warwickshire, to make a herbal tea that is used to alleviate sprains, and in cases of colds and bronchitis.

Edith Sitwell, poet; Eric Coates, composer; Sir Reginald Wingate, empire builder and Governor of Sudan; Sheila Kaye-Smith, novelist; James Hamilton, Third Duke of Abercorn and first Governor of Northern Ireland: these, plus a considerable selection of the aristocracy and the notability formed the Advisory Committee of The Society of Herbalists at the beginning of World War Two.

Anyone who dismisses herbal medicine as a fanciful confidence trick, worked by witchdoctors on hippies and other naive non-conformists, should read this extract from HM Government's Ministry of Agriculture and Fisheries Bulletin No 121, 'Medicinal Herbs and their Cultivation', printed and published by His Majesty's Stationery Office in 1941, price 6d.

The curative properties of drugs, which by simple processes could be extracted from a wide range of plants, have been known by man from the earliest times. Such knowledge accrued through the centuries, until during the 17th century as many as 1,600 different plants were cultivated in some of the famous 'Physic' gardens of the time.

With the advance of scientific knowledge, pharmacy developed into an exact science – a branch of medical science – as distinct from the empirical character of the herbalist's 'remedies', although the source of the substances employed was still the wild or cultivated herbs, or medicinal plants. The present century, however, has seen a considerable development not only of the production of synthetic substances of both organic and inorganic origin, which contain the active principles of the drugs previously obtained from plants, but also of entirely new chemical substances which are successfully used in medical treatment.

Thus, the use of vegetable drugs has declined considerably. Nevertheless, there are still substances of vegetable origin which the drug manufacturer needs. These substances are chiefly of the important group known as alkaloids, of which hyoscyamine of Belladonna (Atropa belladonna) is an outstanding example. Their distribution is comparatively restricted among plants, being found chiefly in the families Rubiaceae, Papaveraceae, Fumariaceae, Solanaceae, Leguminosae and Apocynaceae. The alkaloids are found in all parts of the plants concerned, especially in the leaves and seeds of annuals, the roots and leaves of biennials and in the bark and fruit skins of perennial species. Other plant substances used to a less extent in pharmacy include the glycosides, e.g. the digitalin of Digitalis purpurea, and the ethereal oils, e.g. the oil of Mentha piperita.

The drug manufacturers of this country have relied very considerably on imported supplies of the various medicinal plants they require. These supplies were usually collected from wild growths, or grown chiefly by peasant cultivators. The quantity grown or collected in this country was small by comparison, and although during the last war attempts were made to establish the cultivation of drug-producing plants on a wider scale, little real headway was made, and the effort has since declined. Under the conditions of the present war, however, drug manufacturers find themselves cut off from many of their usual sources of supply, and the following information relating to medicinal plants for which there is an urgent demand, and which can be grown in this country, should be of assistance to those who desire to embark on their cultivation.

Particularly is the further production of belladonna, digitalis, henbane and stramonium to be encouraged; and a scheme under the aegis of the Ministry of Health has been formulated to increase home-grown supplies of these four herbs.

Farmers who wish to undertake cultivation of these herbs should consult their County War Agricultural Executive Committee as to the advisability of carrying such crops on their land. The Wholesale Drug Trade Association, 4 & 5, Queen Square, London, W.C.I, will be pleased to give any necessary advice from the standpoint of suitable production.

The material in this Bulletin has been taken, after some necessary revision, from an earlier publication (Bulletin No. 76, Herbs).

Ministry of Agriculture and Fisheries, February, 1941.

While the Ministry writer is careful to tell potential growers of the poisonous nature of deadly nightshade, there is no such warning connected with stramonium, also known as thorn apple, which is every bit as dangerous with seeds deceptively sweet. Henbane too carries no red flag. Although nobody would be likely to eat its foul-smelling leaves, if they did 'either in sallet or in pottage, then doth it bring frenzie, and whoso useth more than four leaves shall be in danger to sleepe without waking', as one writer of old put it fairly clearly.

As well as nightshade, foxglove, thorn apple and henbane, the Ministry also hoped for commercial-scale cultivators and/or gatherers of opium poppy, valerian, aconite (monk's hood), chamomile, squirting cucumber, autumn crocus and a dozen more, including buckthorn.

Common buckthorn is a shrubby tree not unlike the maple, beset with spines and bearing dull, black berries about the size of elderberries, each containing four seeds. These berries are used to a limited extent and are purchased by manufacturing chemists in some districts, such as Hertfordshire, for the preparation of a purgative syrup.

As the Ministry pointed out, synthetic substances and entirely new drugs had, by 1941, largely displaced the old herbal remedies and, in doing so, destroyed what must have seemed to be permanent kinds of farming, what we might call traditional niche businesses. Pennyroyal:

was probably the first of the mints to be cultivated in this country and for many centuries pennyroyal and the extracted pennyroyal oil were used medicinally. It is used in Yorkshire as an appetizer for cows that have recently calved.

Peppermint has been cultivated for many years in the Mitcham district of Surrey where acreage was once considerable, but is now much reduced. Market Deeping in Lincolnshire and Hitchin in Hertfordshire have also been important centres for this industry.

The juice of the wild lettuce (botanical name *Lactuca virosa*, meaning the lettuce that stinks), useful as a sedative, had been a near monopoly for the citizens of the German town of Zell, their annual production of 150 kilograms being regarded as 'sufficient to meet world requirements'. In wartime, the Ministry was pleased to note, 'it is occasionally cultivated in England, for example, in Hertfordshire'.

No such recourse was available with the dandelion.

Cultivated dandelion, as used in salads, is almost useless, as it is deficient in the active principle for which dandelion is valued. In districts within easy reach of

Dig for victory. Collect a kilo of dandelion roots in 1941 and the local pharmaceuticals factory would give you about seven shillings and sixpence for a hundredweight, the equivalent of £40 in modern purchasing power.

factories it is customary for the country people to dig up dandelion roots during the late summer and autumn months, and to sell them roughly cleaned to the manufacturers, from whom they obtain a price of 5s–8s 6d per cwt.

The chief active principle in dandelion is taraxacin, chemically termed a bitter glycoside, which is to say one of hundreds of substances, such as the digitalin already mentioned by the Ministry, and salicin, the precursor of aspirin. These glycosides occur in plants, have both a sugar and a non-sugar component in the molecule, and generally have an action of some kind on the human system. Taraxacin's action is largely diuretic, hence the many names for the dandelion referring to this feature such as pissimire and pittlebed, although the good folk of Derbyshire used dandelion juice against warts, apparently.

The 'country people' to whom the Ministry referred in 1941 were getting on average about £40 in modern wages equivalent for their hundredweights of roots, or about 80p a kilo, which doesn't seem a lot for the work involved.

Much of our herbal lore was preserved and handed on by the monasteries and nunneries of the middle ages. Those living the monastic life saw the treatment of the sick as their duty and the various effects of herbal treatments were studied with the deepest scholarship. We have to understand that all such medicine and medical practice was based on observation and belief, not on any real understanding of how things worked. No monk or nun would pretend to cure a disease, but only to ease the symptoms. Disease was a product of sin, or of the will of a god who moved in mysterious ways. Only prayer and repentance could bring about a cure, so if a cure resulted from the treatment, that was down to divine intervention, not the Cistercian potion.

The most common speedwell in the UK, the germander speedwell, *Veronica chamaedrys*, was a famous old cure for coughs when made into a syrup. Perhaps the wildest medieval claim for it was as a cure for cancer when mixed with chicken soup.

Meadowsweet, *Filipendula ulmaria*, is sweet all right, smelling gently of almonds, but it doesn't really grow in meadows, preferring ditches and pond-side dampness. In any case, the name comes from its use in flavouring mead; it was called meadwort. Gerard says that 'the smell thereof makes the heart merrie and joyful and delighteth the senses'. Mrs Grieve says 'it is a valuable medicine in diarrhoea, imparting to the bowels some degree of nourishment', and the druids revered it as one of the three most holy herbs.

Curiously, they all rather missed the point of meadowsweet. Its previous Latin name, *Spiraea*, gives us spiraeic acid,* and it was that substance, extracted from meadowsweet flowers and willow bark in the nineteenth century, that eventually led to the discovery of one of the world's most successful drugs, acetylated spiraeic acid, otherwise known as aspirin (*now called salicylic acid, from *salix*, willow).

Medicinally, thyme is not trumpeted in our era, although it used to be described as 'profitable for such as are fearful, melancholic and troubled in mind'. If such a mood should strike, a few minutes spent in the sun contemplating a fine display of thyme might still work. 'Thyme tea will arrest gastric fermentation,' says Mrs Grieve, whatever that may mean, and Culpeper is equally mysterious with his assertion that it will dispel 'any pains and hardness of the spleen'. He also says it 'helps sciatica and dullness of sight', while Gerard gives it as a cure for 'sciatica and pains in the head', although the main claim is for a treatment of whooping cough and sore throats.

The knapweeds were classed as vulnaries, that is, of use in healing wounds, their roots and seeds being included in the preparation of ointments. Before and after flowering, this is *Centaurea nigra*, the lesser knapweed, also called hardheads, probably the most common of them. There is also *C. scabiosa*, greater knapweed, which is bigger and with dandelion-style leaves, and *C. nemoratis*, the brown knapweed, a more slender version of *nigra*, found mostly in the south. Culpeper recommends making a decoction to cure your sore throat and your nosebleeds.

Opposite: Feverfew, *Tanacetum parthenium*, is sometimes recommended for the perfumed garden, although not everyone likes the perfume. That includes bees, which avoid it, a feature that fits well with one of its ancient uses as an insect repellent. The fresh herb rubbed on the skin will relieve insect bites, while an infusion made from it is said to cure a cold and cure a fever and, according to Mrs Grieve, 'will afford relief to the face-ache or earache of a dyspeptic or rheumatic person'. Perhaps Guy Fawkes and others who were sent to the Tower at the King's pleasure took a supply of feverfew with them, since it will also 'allay any distressing sensitiveness to pain in a highly nervous subject'.

An ounce of ground ivy, *Glechoma hederacea*, made into a pint of tea, is an old remedy for a persistent headache – other remedies having been tried and found wanting, presumably, or the headache would not have persisted. The same tea will also help your melancholy, should that state proceed from stoppings in your spleen.

This plant, which has nothing to do with ivy except that its leaves look a little like it, has another name: alehoof. 'The women of our Northern parts, especially Wales and Cheshire, do turn Herbe-Ale-hoof into their ale, but the reason I know not.' The reason, dear Gerard, is that it helps clarify the ale and gives it better keeping qualities. Some would say it also makes it taste better, and some would not say that. Anyway, as with costmary/alecost, when brewing ceased to be the duty of every housewife and became instead a matter for commercial breweries, ground ivy was soon pushed out by the more prolific, easier to gather, better at its job, hops.

Credited with healing powers against snakebite, the ribwort plantain, *Plantago lanceolata*, is one of our most widespread and plentiful wild herbs. It has much the same qualities as the equally common or great plantain, *P. major*. The leaves can be eaten when young, preferably cooked, but are better employed on cuts and scrapes, stings and scalds. The seeds are a laxative but tea made from the leaves has the opposite effect and may also ease the discomfort of piles.

Plantain was one of the Anglo-Saxons' nine sacred herbs; they called it *wegbrade*, journey- or way-bread, and, along with many peoples before and after them, put it in just about every kind of medicine.

The nine herbs that were proof against poison, provided they were mixed together with the appropriate magic spell, were mucgwyrt (mugwort), wegbrade (plantain), stune (hairy bittercress), atorlathe (venom-loather, betony), mægthe (mayweed, stinking chamomile), stithe (nettle), wergulu (crabapple), fille (thyme) and finule (fennel).

Hoary plantain, also called lamb's tongue, *Plantago media*, spreads its large, oval leaves flat on the ground to preserve its position against all-comers. It throws up this attractive spike of minute flowers with pale purple filaments, often resulting in a more pink effect than here, where the flower is a quite startling white. The plant is supposed to have an affinity with apple and pear trees, both of which can suffer from apple canker, a fungus that destroys bark on branches. Hoary plantain leaves rubbed on the wounds are said to kill the fungus and help with healing.

All the bindweeds are purgatives and that has been their main use in medicine. This is the ground creeper, the field bindweed, *Convolvulus arvensis*, which is smaller and more shy and retiring than its blatant big white cousin, *C. sepium*. Both close their flowers when the sun shines not; the little pink field one also closes during sunshine and showers. *C. sepium* is well known for climbing anti-clockwise, which is also counter to the daily direction of the sun in the northern hemisphere, but so does the runner bean, which comes from the southern hemisphere.

Field pennycress, *Thlaspi arvense*, also called mithridate mustard, was an ingredient in the complex and ancient antidote to poison supposedly formulated by King Mithridates (see page 19). The Latin *arvense/arvensis* etc. is from *arare*, to plough, and so when applied to plants means that they tend to grow on cultivated land.

Yellow sorrel, *Oxalis corniculata*, is a miniature beauty that can conquer an entire garden, or a village come to that, unless it is kept under close supervision. It is not a native but has made itself at home and, because of its acidic leaves, has been given the common sorrel name although not at all related. Oxalic acid is the reason why one should not eat rhubarb leaves; in yellow sorrel it is only sufficient to give the attractive, if rather small, foliage a salad enlivening quality, providing one doesn't have too much. Medicinal uses are as a coolant in fever and as a blood cleanser.

Wort scare

The Reverend Keble Martin lists nine main species of St John's wort, *Hypericum spp.*, growing wild in the British Isles: perforate, square stalked, wavy, creeping, narrow leaved, beautiful, hairy, mountain and bog. There is also obtuse St John's wort, and the closely related Rose of Sharon, and a few more rare ones.

The one with the herbal tradition is *H. perforatum*, perforate St John's wort, and herein lies a modern herbal tale. Amid much media hype, extract of St John's wort was hailed as an answer to those scourges of today, depression and anxiety. There was some history in this, the ancients having believed it to banish evil spirits and therefore to be effective in treating those possessed by same, that is, the mentally ill, the depressed and the anxious.

The facts of the case are quite simple. Preparations of St John's wort have been shown to be of some benefit in mild depression but – and it's a serious 'but' – the herb also reacts with drugs already being taken for depression and for other, possibly more serious, illnesses, mental and physical. The official medical advice is: do not take St John's wort if you are already on medication, and certainly not without checking with your doctor.

How to make a stringent gargle

Put the following ingredients into a very clean earthen pipkin: twenty sage leaves, a handful of red rose leaves, and a pint of water; boil these for twenty minutes, then add a gill of vinegar, and two tablespoonfuls of honey; boil again for ten minutes, and strain the gargle through a muslin bag, to be used when cold. *A Plain Cookery Book for the Working Classes*, Charles Elmé Francatelli, Chief Cook to HM Queen Victoria.

The forget-me-nots of wood and field, *Myosotis sylvatica* and *M. arvensis*, members of the borage tribe, are supposed to be effective in lung disease, having been made into a syrup. The name was given to the flower, apparently, because of the romantic inclinations of a particularly chivalrous knight. He, picking flowers for his beloved on the river bank, fell into the water. While most people would have shouted 'Help!' and cursed their earlier decision to wear armour for flower picking, this fellow shouted 'Forget me not' as he drowned.

Herbs for Ill Health

Cuckoo pint, *Arum maculatum*, comes in various guises, spotted and not spotted. In any case, unless you want to make a rather tasteless sort of psuedo-milkshake, keep off. Also known as 'lords and ladies', this is a plant to be treated with care. All visible parts – leaves, mini-bullrush-style flower and red berries – are poisonous, and the berries very much so. If taken unawares, you will suffer irritation, both external and internal, and may well find out why its ancient use as a purgative fell out of favour, it being considered too violent.

The root, although poisonous also, can be rendered harmless by cooking, the usual practice being to roast and grind to a powder, whereupon you have a thickening agent that was regularly used as a second choice for sago and arrowroot. More interestingly, cuckoo pint was also a wild, home-grown substitute for a group of exotic Turkish orchids collectively known as salep, the powdered roots of which made a sweetish, thickened drink still popular in Turkey but displaced in Britain by coffee and tea. Charles Lamb thought salep a delicate and refined beverage and recommended it as a breakfast on which to go to work, especially with a slice of bread and butter.

Dog's mercury, *Mercurialis perennis*, is said to be an indicator of ancient, undisturbed woodland, but really it can get everywhere except where the soil is acid. Its poison is also said to be destroyed by drying, but not by cooking, as those mistaking it for good king Henry have sometimes found out. It is so, so plentiful in early spring that we must think it has a use but it is quite capable of causing death in the young or infirm.

No member of the buttercup family (*Ranunculaceae*) should come to the table. Lesser celandine can be plentiful in dampish woods in early spring but it's no go, and doubly so with that dog's mercury.

Related to dog's mercury but rather more dangerous are the spurges, the *Euphorbiaceae*. Charlemagne's recommended species was the caper spurge, *Euphorbia lathyris*, which in the UK lives mainly in southerly woods and gardens, but please do not mistake its seed capsules for capers. The processed seeds express a clear oil, the Oil of Euphorbia, a violently purgative poison; a few seeds on their own won't kill you but they will do more for you than any amount of syrup of figs.

Pictured is the sun spurge, *E. helioscopia*, looking rather spooky in close-up but common enough where the ground is cultivated, also called seven sisters and wart spurge. Sun spurge does have high repute for wart removal but it can irritate the skin too and acts as a powerful astringent.

Readers may well buy a spurge every year without knowing it. *E. pulcherrima*, in Latin the most beautiful euphorbia, we know as the poinsettia.

A full list of poisonous plants is impractical in this work. Common sense says you are not going to eat the large amounts of bracken and apple pips necessary to put you in hospital, nor are you likely, when staggering through a bog in Devon, to feel an irresistible desire to eat a five-feet-tall hemlock water dropwort. Once you know that columbine/aquilegia is buttercup family you won't eat it, and you won't fancy ivy, privet or monkshood. You know about mistletoe. Things called henbane and cowbane don't exactly encourage kitchen experiments.

Most of the plants that look and smell all right are all right, and most of those are not worth eating anyway. Anything that has an unpleasant odour, such as dog's mercury, you will throw aside, but if you are going to get semi-serious about free greens, do arm yourself with a proper field guide.

Chapter Seven

Food for Bees and People

The Bee and Butterfly Garden

This is a particular variety of thyme called pink ripple, but bees do not discriminate. They like all thymes.

Buying an old house for renovation is a risky business, especially when you know nothing at all about old houses and renovating them. In the case of a fifteenth-century half-timbered house which, over the years, had had several more modern houses placed inside it, the risk was even greater because you could see virtually nothing of the original building except the roof timbers.

These seemed to sag rather. Your correspondent learned later that they would have supported a thatch at first, and the subsequent change to pottery pantiles had increased their burden to sagging point. The sky could be seen through little gaps in the pantiles, and when it snowed that winter there was a thick carpet in the attic, but never mind, worse was to come.

The house was in four bays, that is, in the ceilings on both floors it had three main beams running across the width – which was, as is the case with most such houses of the non-aristocratic sort, about eighteen feet. And here lay the first bit of worse to come.

Fashion in housing through the ages is a fascinating business and in every century people, who do not change, have set going their own equivalent of modern trends.

Nowadays we put stone facings on brick council houses as soon as we own instead of rent them. We consider it stylish to have deliberate bobbly bits in the middle of window panes, when they – the panes with the glass blower's mark – used to be considered the worst and would have been thrown away if glass had not been so dear.

In the 1950s we faced panelled doors, painted as they were meant to be, with hardboard and replaced the old brass knobs with aluminium handles. In the 1980s we ripped off the hardboard, stripped the paint off the doors in hot caustic and put the brass knobs back on again.

Our forefathers did the same. Fifteenth- and sixteenth-century houses had ceilings which were only the underside of the floorboards above, laid on joists. The floorboards and joists could never deteriorate because they were constantly smoked by the fire and were open to draughts and light. The fire, by the way, would have been in an open hearth with the smoke going out through a hole in the roof.

Merchants and others of the middle class who had these houses began to think it was a bit common to live like this, so they built fireplaces and chimneys. Once the false walls were removed, that had surrounded the chimney in the house being described, it was clear that renovation was not the right word. The demolition of the entire chimney would be necessary. It was leaning and lurching. It would have to be taken down, brick by brick, saving the bricks – beautiful old soft reds – for use in the new rebuilt model.

Scaffolding was placed around the chimney stack on the roof. Work would start at the top, naturally, lowering the carefully removed bricks down the chimney in a rubber bucket on a rope. The weather was glorious. Up there on the roof, with a view of the whole town and the countryside beyond to a brilliant blue and green horizon, what could be more exhilarating? The work certainly wasn't hard, no more than was the mortar holding the bricks together. There was some evidence of half-hearted attempts at pointing, but mostly it was just the old lime mortar, now so soft that bricks lifted off with bare hands.

As your correspondent did this, occasionally stopping to admire the vista or to tap a mildly recalcitrant brick with a hammer, he noticed that many of the layers of mortar had little tunnels in them. These tunnels seemed to be lined with a transparent, crinkly, thin substance like old Cellophane, and they had yellow powder in them. The writer, much younger then, didn't know what they were, and anyway how could he be concerned with such matters? He was demolishing a chimney. A new chimney, even better than the old one, was to be built, a magnificent ingle-nook fireplace would result, and the fifteenth-century half-timbered merchant's house would have back the fire it deserved.

No more would the residents of this historic building huddle in front of a ridiculous 1950s brown tile job with a letter rack and a clock on the mantlepiece and flying ducks on the wall above it.

Butterflies too like thyme. You really can't be without it.

African blue basil has – to us at any rate – a quite strong smell of camphor, which you might think would put insects off. As this busy bee shows, matters are quite the reverse.

Looks attractive but, to us, smells rather unpleasant, the hedge woundwort, here growing in a garden, is a magnet for bumble bees. They are very adept at climbing inside those flowers, which have white target indicators for accurate bee guidance.

The dismantler set to his dismantling with more gusto then ever and, as the sun began to set, he reached his first goal, which was to demolish down to the level of the roof ridge. It was a big chimney, and this represented many hundreds of bricks removed and lowered in the rubber bucket, and a good day's work.

How lovely everything looked as the shades began to creep and the sun ripened its colour. What a difference this was, living here instead of Shepherd's Bush. Yes, this was what life was all about. A summer's rural evening, a setting sun, a day's reasonably tiring physical work, a clear difference made, and a pint or three afterwards.

Then it became apparent what all those little tunnels were. Just as the rim of the sun touched the horizon, about twenty bees turned up. They hovered, stationary but for their wing beats, their questing antennae pointing towards the empty space where the chimney and their tunnels had been. They were homeless, and they couldn't understand.

There were several different sorts, some quite big bumbly ones and some smaller, but they were all solitary bees and they had come home to find that, while they were out on their own legitimate business, someone had knocked their houses down.

After a while, maybe fifteen minutes, they realised that their houses were not going to materialise. They turned, one by one, and flew away. Your man turned too, suddenly sad. He climbed down the scaffolding and went to the pub.

Compared to the strains put on bee populations these days, this was a very minor blip indeed. Everywhere that humankind progresses, bees seem to suffer and their importance to life on earth becomes, briefly, a great cause for concern. It is an old story, but we don't seem to learn from it. The first five-year plan adopted by the new Soviet Union forced the development of large collective farms out of the small, peasant-style holdings of previous eras. Bee nesting places were much reduced and seed production fell dramatically and at once. The same thing had already happened in Germany during the First World War, when bee keeping was forgotten in favour of seemingly more urgent matters.

Even with these lessons, we still spray insecticides indiscriminately and destroy bee habitat without a thought. For the gardener, no bees would mean no garden, or at least a garden with little variety, as only a few types of plant can self-fertilise, so it's in all our interests to encourage bees as much as we can.

Bees will be bees. You do all you can for them, growing all kinds of special bee-attracting plants, and they buzz off looking for dandelions, clover and hogweed. Well, they like pretty well all the *Compositae* and *Umbelliferae* tribes.

Herbs for bees include birdsfoot trefoil, bee balm of course, bee orchid, betony, borage, bugle, catmint and all the mints and dead-nettles, chicory, clover, comfrey, cornflower, cranesbill, evening primrose, heliotrope, hyssop, knapweed, lavender, lungwort, rose, rosemary, sage, scabious, thistle, thyme, valerian, verbena, witch hazel, woodruff, woundwort, yarrow and yellow rattle.

The bee orchid, *Ophrys apifera*, has one of the most elaborate fertilisation strategies, yet it doesn't seem to work too well. The bottom half of the flower looks, to a male bumblebee anyway, just like the female of his dreams. It smells right too, as the flower sends out the proper pheromones to get him going. He tries to mate with it, gets his head covered in pollen, eventually falls off in frustration, goes to the next flower and passes on the pollen.

The logical conclusion of all this would be a decline in the bumblebee population while bee orchids increased beyond measure, but that is not the case. Bee orchids are quite rare some years, more plentiful others, while the male bumblebee carries on regardless. The flower can, and often does, self-fertilise, a quality that makes it highly suitable for the bee garden, if its stunning looks were not enough.

Red valerian, *Centranthus ruber*, is not a native of Britain but it has certainly settled in. It actively dislikes good ground, much preferring cracks in walls. Although the leaves are just about edible, the main reason for growing it is its beauty and its great attraction to insects, especially butterflies.

The pyramidal orchid, *Anacamptis pyramidalis*, may be lovely to look at but it's certainly not heaven to kiss, smelling quite strongly of something sweet but repulsive. Butterflies and bees clearly do not share our distaste because they flock to it.

The common or lesser knapweed, *Centaurea nigra* of the *Compositae*, not to be confused with the centauries, which are gentians, shows nothing but small brown knobs until the weather warms up. Then, around the middle of June in southern districts, around the longest day in Suffolk, these brilliant purple thistle-like heads burst forth, much to the delight of the local bees.

Not everyone wants ivy crawling around the place but growing it on a lowish wall or trellis will get it to flower when it reaches the top. These flowers are late in the year and, for the bees that are still about, provide one of the few sources of nectar. The black berries are also a last resort food for birds, such as thrushes and blackbirds, in a bad winter.

Herbs can have an effect on the rest of the garden, too. Said to repel rather than kill insect pests are quite a lot of herbs including hyssop, rosemary, sage, thyme, feverfew and rue. The method is to make up some strong herb tea. Fill a measuring vessel with the bruised or chopped leaves of the named herb or herbs, tip into a larger jug, fill the same measuring vessel with boiling water, tip on to the herbs when just off the boil, leave to mash. Dilute with one vesselful of cold water, add a squeeze of washing-up liquid, and there's your spray. Try it. Keep notes.

Among the herbs supposed to act as living deterrents, coriander is a convenient quick grower and, if the scent of battle lights your eye, you could put pot-planted rosemary, sage and members of the mint family upwind of your carrots on those sunny May days when the carrot fly is looking for somewhere to lay her eggs. On no account use parsley for this job; it will have the opposite effect. Another of the parsley family, chervil, is said to ward off slugs and snails, although how this can be tested and proved is hard to guess.

Herbs for the Kitchen

The young leaves of borage were always considered good to eat and were a frequent ingredient in salads, among that class of person which made and ate salads. Possibly the finest borage salad is the medicinal one that goes into Pimm's No 1 Cup: lemon slice, strawberry slices, mint leaves and borage leaves. Some people would add cucumber but the borage does that job. Long before the invention of Pimm's, borage steeped in wine was alleged to bring about total amnesia. Such an effect can still be observed, despite the weakening of the aforementioned Cup since its inception, simply by adding gin.

Lemon verbena, *Aloysia citrodora*, can be used in any dish instead of lemon balm. It's a much bigger plant than the balm and so gives a richer harvest but, being a South American native, it needs some protection against frost.

Frances Bardswell writes:

> In the course of last July, while we were in the midst of enjoying the aromatic
> pleasures of our garden of Herbs, then greatly in perfection, we were pleased to
> notice in the pages of a well-known weekly periodical a pleasant and useful
> column devoted entirely to the subject of culinary Herbs and their cultivation.
> We are entirely in sympathy with what is said, especially in the idea of using
> Parsley as an edging plant; it is what we frequently do ourselves, thereby
> imitating the Greek gardeners of old, who had such a habit of bordering their
> gardens with Parsley and Rue that a saying arose when an undertaking was
> contemplated, but not yet commenced, 'Oh, we are only at the Parsley and Rue.'

The useful column was by Donald McDonald in *The Queen* magazine, issue of 30 July
1910. It is the tendency of all factual writers, gardening and otherwise, to reinvent the
wheel every so often, and to present to a new audience a selection of elderly
information as if it were of itself innovative, when it is only the readership that is new
to it. This factual writer will resist the temptation and present to you the article in
question, written a whole century ago. No amendments are deemed necessary.

> A garden of herbs – there is savouriness in the very name. And yet often the
> most unsatisfactory things in gardens, especially small ones, are the herbs.
> Scattered here and there all over the place, they have mostly a ragged, neglected
> look, and are very often not to be found when wanted; and if they are, time and
> patience are probably exhausted in hunting them up when wanted in a hurry for
> flavouring. Quite a pleasing feature might be made in even a small garden of the
> herbs were they only brought together and arranged in order.
>   The best position for herbs is in beds, and these may be made from two or
> four feet wide, with foot alleys between them, and the length at the least one
> third more than the width. This disposition in beds is so much more convenient
> and better in appearance than rows at regular intervals, which remind one more
> of herb-growing for medicines or perfumes, not of gatherings and snippings for
> culinary purposes. In small gardens one entire bed will not be needed for any
> one herb, and in them several may be grown together in one bed, such for
> instance, as common and lemon thyme, pennyroyal, and marjoram in one;
> fennel, sage, and tarragon in another; and basil, summer savory, and golden
> purslane together. Mint should have a bed to itself, as mint sauce is always in
> demand, and almost everyone likes it with lamb and for flavouring peas. Chervil,
> too, is often required for salads. Some may also desire to reserve a bed for

angelica, for the luxury of its young shoots candied in sugar, and the growth of borage, for the flavouring of claret cups.

Again, the herb garden is just the place for the systematic cultivation of small salading, such as a succession of young onions, a bed of chives, radishes, rampion, lettuce, endive. All these would furnish a good many beds, and by changing those that are not permanent for different products, a nice succession of cropping might be maintained. A parsley bed or beds must not be omitted, for nothing is more useful in a household, alike for flavouring or garnishing, and it is just as easy on a right system to have fine leaves, exquisitely curled and clean, because raised high above the ground by their strength of stature, as to have and use the small dirty leaves that have to do duty as parsley in many households. Let the parsley have a bed of rich, deep soil; sow the best curled seed thinly; as soon as up thin the plants to six inches apart, and then let them grow away freely. That is the whole art of growing and using parsley, and making it one of the finest foliaged plants in the garden. Sow in July for succession. If the garden of herbs is too small for the devotion of one or more beds to parsley sown at different seasons, then the whole herb-garden might be fringed round with it, and the flowering plants themselves be garnished with its beauty.

Sage is one of the most useful of garden herbs, and may be grown from either seeds or cuttings. Spring is the usual season for sowing the seeds, although they can be put in now in a shady spot and firm soil. Cuttings may also be taken out now, choosing those shoots that do not show a flower head at the top; they will root steadily in a fairly moist soil, and unless the sun is very bright will not need any shading. I have seen gardeners put a spadeful or two of earth into the heart of a sage bush, and the growths thus covered soon take root; they are then separated from the old bush and planted alone.

Thyme – both common and lemon – is another herb much in request for culinary requirements. It may be raised from seeds or cuttings or by dividing the plant. An open position is essential, as full exposure to the air increases the aromatic properties, much of which is lost when the plant is smothered up with other things. For keeping purposes thyme should be cut when at the height of its flowering.

Of mint several varieties are grown, but the spearmint is the most useful. Mint does not produce seeds in our climate, but is easily increased by cuttings made of pieces of the creeping underground stems, which grow freely when supplied with plenty of moisture. During summer, when the stems are full of juice, is the best time to gather mint to dry for winter use.

No portion of a garden, large or small, will afford more pleasure than the herb garden when it is well kept and furnished. There will always be something growing and doing in it, and when divided in the manner stated the different parts are so easily managed that a bed may be dug or sown at any spare moment.

Of course, if you grow herbs for the kitchen you will want to preserve your surplus in high season for those times when everything is dank and cold and a hot dish with summer flavours is required. Those unlucky folk who have no herbs growing must repair to the grocer's shop and buy, at enormous expense, little glass jars or plastic packets of mechanically chopped and dried herbs which, we cannot deny, often bear resemblance to those we grow but, quite honestly, nobody with any option would buy them. Here is Miss Sinclair Rohde on the subject:

> Home dried herbs are vastly superior to those sold in packets. To secure well flavoured herbs for winter use they should be gathered before they flower and after the dew dries off them, but before the sun is at its hottest. It is essential to dry in shade and as quickly as possible. Hanging the herbs tied in small, loose bunches in a hot attic with a current of air blowing through is ideal. Failing the hot attic, any warm room will do almost as well and it is better to hang up the herbs than to spread them out on tables. If spreading on tables is the only possible way, they should be spread as thinly as possible, and turned at least twice a day. In a very wet summer it is sometimes necessary to dry in the oven, but this must be done at a very low temperature. The best way is to remove the oven shelves, and balance rods across, resting the ends on the shelf supports. From these rods, the bunches of herbs can be suspended.

We cannot know what sort of oven Miss S R had in 1936 but balancing rods across it does sound a rather tricky way of doing things. Your correspondent would add, if the lady Eleanour will allow, that it is a very good idea to encase your bunches of herbs in paper bags, tied loosely at the top. The method previously employed was to hang the bunches over the Rayburn – or it could be an Aga – just like they do for the photographs of rural, cottagey bliss in those magazines devoted to the urban dream. This worked very well but, having left the bunches there a little too long, taking them down resulted in a shower of small autumn leaves and the loss of half the crop behind the stove.

Herby lamb pilau. For two people: cut a boned breast of lamb, or the equivalent in lamb shoulder, into conveniently sized pieces, an inch or so square. Place in a good strong pot, such as a cast-iron casserole, on a medium heat while you slice up an onion small and gather a goodly handful of mint from your garden, plus about three inches of rosemary. Add the onion, rosemary leaves and chopped mint to the pot, with a splash of orange juice.

The fat in the lamb should be enough to lubricate the cooking; if not, add some butter or oil. Add a heaped teaspoon of ground coriander seed, two of paprika, and half or more of chilli powder. Turn the heat down and cook for an hour. Add more juice or water to prevent sticking. At the end there should be just enough thick liquid to permeate the cooked basmati rice that you are going to stir in. Serve with a simple vegetable curry and strewn with fresh coriander leaves.

Old-fashioned lemonade is a delight of summer, whether you add anything stronger to it or not. Mint lemonade is even better. You need a good handful of mint leaves, but not eau-de-cologne or peppermint. Use garden mint or apple mint. Put in your blender with two dessertspoons of white caster sugar and a cup of water. Give a quick whizz, pour into a jug, add the juice of three lemons and top up with cold water to two pints, or a litre and a bit. Serve with ice and mint leaves.

If you don't have a blender, pour a cup or so of boiling water on your chopped mint leaves and leave to cool before dissolving the sugar and adding the lemon. A variation is to top up with soda water. Or, miss out the sugar, top up with tonic water and use as a mixer with gin or vodka.

Jelly mint lamb. You can do this with left-over lamb, if it can be cut into big thick slices, or start from scratch with some chops or a piece of rolled shoulder. In any case you want to end up with a nice arrangement of good-sized pieces of cooked lamb in a serving dish with sides, such as a lasagne dish.

   Make up a quantity of liquid from a good, appley cider pressed from real apples, a little lemon juice, a little sugar, and strong mint tea (as in the first stage of mint sauce). You want enough to cover the lamb completely. Measure your liquid; refer to the instructions on a packet of gelatine for the correct amount, do what it says and pour your jelly over your lamb. Leave to cool and set.

Epping sausages. Put about a pound each of minced pork and suet into a bowl, with a handful of finely chopped herbs, being thyme, savory, marjoram and sage together, and the rind of half a lemon grated. Season with salt, pepper, and nutmeg or cinnamon. Work the mixture until blended well, adding beaten egg as necessary. Make into patty or sausage shapes and fry gently.

Easter herb pudding. This is another traditional recipe with as many variations as there are villages in the north of England. The main green ingredient is usually the leaves of bistort, *Polygonum bistorta*, also called snakeweed, that grows in wet upland pastures such as they have in Pennine districts, but any combination can become your own version – nettles, dandelion, hedge garlic, wild garlic, ground ivy, alexanders and so on. This wild garlic was growing by the Cleddau estuary in Pembrokeshire.

Take a handful of pearl barley and soak it overnight. Add a handful of oatmeal, season, and mix in your greens, finely chopped, a couple of pounds or so (a kilo-ish), and a beaten egg. Steam for an hour or two in a greased pudding basin and turn out to serve, historically with the first meat after Lent.

Cambridge spring soup (traditional). Shell enough peas to get about a pint. Chop onions and a good bunch each of parsley, sorrel, chervil and purslane. Put all together in a pot with butter and water over a moderate fire until softened, and pass the whole through a fine sieve. Make a thick sauce with egg yolks and milk, stir in the sieved vegetables and serve when all is hot.

Norfolk dumplings. Next time you make a stew, or a casserole if you're slightly upmarket, put in some Norfolk herb dumplings for the last half hour of cooking. A dish of rabbit and bacon, in the pot with whatever vegetables you might have, would be appropriate. The basic dumpling recipe is two of self-raising flour to one of suet, seasoned with salt and a certain mustard powder from Norwich, plus large amounts of chopped herbs. Hedge garlic, chives and parsley make a good combination. Add water to make a softish dough and roll into balls about the size of a bantam's egg, or a golf ball.

Nettle beer. Enough here for a brew. Cheers, all. This is a fizzy, summer drink, not for keeping. To a gallon of water, or five litres, add two pounds or a kilo of nettle tops and leaves and boil for a quarter of an hour or so. Strain the liquor into your brewing vessel – pot or plastic – and add a pound or half a kilo of brown sugar and an ounce or thirty grams of cream of tartar.

When cool, stir to make sure all the sugar is dissolved and add the juice of two lemons. Add beer yeast (started according to instructions) or sprinkle some fresh yeast from the baker. Cover and leave to ferment in a warm place for four or five days; you want it to be just about worked out but not quite.

Decant or siphon the beer into strong plastic bottles that have previously held carbonated drinks. Check occasionally. If any seems about to explode, let off a little pressure with the screwtop. Mature for a week; serve cold.

Cowslip wine. A wildflower recipe from the eighteenth century is not feasible in our herbicidal days, but a much-scaled-down version of it might be tried with clover, dandelion and other plentiful flowers. The main point is to avoid getting any stems into the concoction.

Boil 20 gallons of water for quarter of an hour. Add 50 pounds of loaf sugar and boil until scum ceases to rise and the liquor is clear. Cool, pour into a tub and add yeast. After a day, add 32 quarts of cowslip flowers. After two more days, pour all into a barrel and add the grated peel of a dozen each of oranges and lemons. Make a syrup with the juice thereof and two pounds of loaf sugar, and set aside in a jar to keep. When your wine has ceased working, add the syrup to it and stop up your barrel well. After three months, your wine will be ready for bottling.

Of course, water from a tap will not need fifteen minutes at a rolling boil to sterilise it, nor should your sugar make scum. While enjoying such benefits of modern living, few people alive today will be able to imagine 32 quarts of cowslip flowers or the meadows they were growing in. Easier will be: one gallon clover flowers, one gallon water, juice and peel of two lemons and two oranges, three pounds of sugar, plus yeast.

The last word on tea

Teas are too often composed of some kind of leaf more or less resembling the real plant, without any of its genuine fragrance, and are, from their spurious and almost poisonous nature, calculated to produce evil to all who consume them, besides the drawback of their being expensive articles.

Teas made from sage leaves, dried mint, marigolds, and more particularly the leaf of the blackcurrant tree, form a very pleasant as well as wholesome kind of beverage; and, if used in equal proportions, would be found to answer very well as a most satisfactory substitute for bad and expensive tea.

A Plain Cookery Book for the Working Classes,
Charles Elmé Francatelli, Chief Cook to HM Queen Victoria.

And Finally, Herbs for Magic

Cuckoo flower, lady's smock or milkmaids, *Cardamine pratensis*, is cress/rocket family with flowers varying from white to mauve. The leaves can be eaten as a more peppery substitute for watercress. It likes wet and boggy places, is attractive to butterflies and is early into flower, usually beating the first cuckoo by a few days, and so would be excellent for your garden if you had such a damp patch. Possibly even more important, it is a magnet for fairies – however, beware. The fairies don't like you picking it and you must not take it into the house nor include it in a May garland.

Creeping cinquefoil has always been closely associated with love potions and amorous divinations, but perhaps its most dramatic use is as an ingredient in an ointment put together by witches and called at the time green ointment or green oil, but these days often given as flying ointment.

Cinquefoil and other, usually much more toxic, herbs were mixed with flour and kneaded with fat. The result was smeared on the body and gave the witch the ability to fly. Possibly some recipes included hallucinogenic and/or soporific herbs, which produced some sort of out-of-body experience and hence the flying legend.

Incidentally, the most effective fat to use for ointment making is the fat of a child recently dead and dug up from its grave at midnight, when the moon is new. Otherwise, use Cookeen or ordinary lard or dripping. For more healthy flying, use Flora.

Rosemary was a symbol of fidelity and friendship and featured at weddings and funerals. Lavender too warded evil spirits away from festive occasions. Both are key ingredients in Four Thieves' Vinegar, a potion meant to prevent you catching the plague, and in a gypsy magic spell to defeat frigidity, thus.

Take lemon balm, rosemary, lavender and sage, dry them, and grind in a mortar. On the night of the new moon, undress with your lover, throw the herb mixture on the fire, and make love on the hearthrug. As you lie together, both of you say:

You herbs of love bring power anew,
May strains and stress be far and few.
Conjoin two hearts so love may flow
To end for e'er our nights of woe.

Do this every night until it is no longer necessary.

Excuse me? Every night? So how do you tell when it is no longer necessary? How many new moons are there? Are you really expecting a couple, one lusty and the other cool, to recite birthday-card-type silly words, in unison, while romping on the Readicut? Seeing as one of them's frigid, how do you persuade ... Oh, never mind. They'll probably do it on the wrong night anyway, because hardly anyone knows that the moon is new when you can't see it at all.

While everyone knows, or should know, that hemlock is poisonous, few may be aware
that magical powers can be conferred upon one wishing to be a magus if, among
other things, his knife with the black hilt is dipped in the juice thereof. That is, always
providing that the knife was made during the hour and day of Saturn, and the juice in
question is mixed with the blood of a black cat.

These two designs for herb gardens, by the much revered Eleanour Sinclair Rohde, should perhaps have carried some sort of warning such as 'Don't try this at home.' If the lady Eleanour seriously contemplated anyone following her main design, then it would have to have been someone with lots of space and several full-time gardeners. Nobody would plant chives as an edging without the resources to keep them constantly in check, and how many plants would you need in the more modest proposal below for thyme walks and lavender borders? Anchusa, by the way, is another name for alkanet.

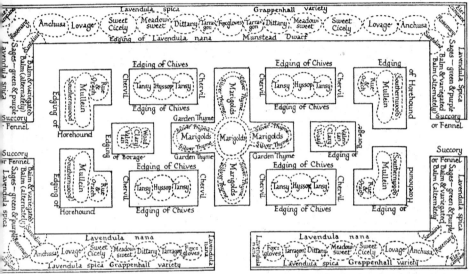

Plan for a Herb Garden with the stately herbs in the outer beds, bordered on either side with Lavenders; the herbs of middle growth in the inner beds & in the centre a Knot garden of Marigolds and Garden Thymes. + + +

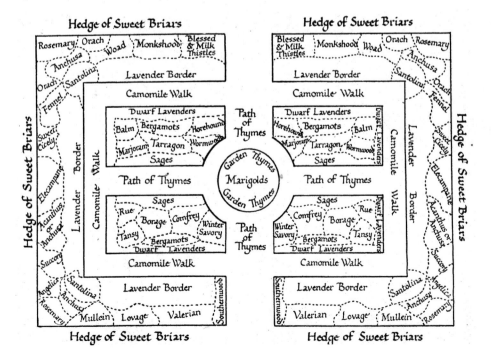